AFRICA
THE WAY FORWARD

AFRICA
THE WAY FORWARD

Canice Chucks Osuji

To order additional copies of this book, contact:
Xlibris
800-056-3182
www.Xlibrispublishing.co.uk
Orders@Xlibrispublishing.co.uk
772997

CONTENTS

DEDICATION

This work is dedicated to the citizens of the great continent of Africa who have been victims of bad governance throughout the centuries.

ACKNOWLEDGEMENTS

I appreciate the efforts and support of my entire family who have been behind me all these years.

I am also grateful for the support and hard work of Hendrick Arbella and his team at Xlibris Publishing UK.

Great thanks go to Almighty Jehovah, who has helped me through all the difficult times and kept me alive despite all odds, especially the tough times I faced in the West.

My appreciation also goes to all friends and well-wishers.

INTRODUCTION

The lack of progress, development, invention, and innovation, coupled with political and religious instability, of the great continent of Africa has limited her from moving forward compared with other continents of the world.

However, these negatives have in a way dominated the story of Africa in the recent centuries. Many around the world know nothing about Africa except hunger, war, and the animals while the great people of Africa are forgotten.

Africa's immense history and culture have influenced the world. A lot of historians have accredited Africa as the place where civilisation started, citing Egypt as an example with its long ages of civilised background or history. In the present day, the continent of Africa is populated with about 960,000,000 inhabitants despite the effects of the lost generation of about 400,000,000 of her children to slavery.

The continent of Africa can't be jettisoned in its position in history regardless of her dark history and the underdevelopment facing her. There is still hope that the continent of Africa can move forward if her people and leaders look back at her history. This will make her discover who they were and then will help them recover.

G. Elliot Smith in the second edition of *The Ancient Egyptians and the Origin of Civilization* said, 'The Egyptians did a great deal more than merely invent agriculture and devise the earliest statecraft and religion. Not only did they devise the methods of working wood and stone and the art of architecture, they seem also to have been the inventors of linen and of the craft of weaving, of the use of gold and copper and the making of metal tools and implements.'

They were the first people to measure the year and to devise a calendar and, later on, to substitute for the rough calculation based upon the date of the annual Nile flood the actual measurement based on observation of the sun's movements. They also invented shipbuilding and constructed the first seagoing ships. In fact, Smith was kind and honest to mention these attributes of the early African achievements because they are hardly remembered today since the African continent is seen as nothing but darkness by the informed and uninformed people of other continents. (See pages 48–49 of *The Growth of Civilization*.)

The idea of the West seeing Africans as people of no inventive acumen isn't something new since credits are given to those who added the last link to discovery, which has been made by groups of men. However, people like Imhotep of Egypt, if he were still alive, would have been more than Albert Einstein; and of course, he would have received the Nobel Prize since he merited it by today's Western standards of honour.

Africans should not give up but should go back to the drawing board in unity despite religious and language differences as well as a Western-induced mentality, which has divided Africa in terms of colonial impacts—a characteristic that has hindered us from aspiring and reinventing ourselves as great sons of the sun.

The first university in Western Europe, University of Salamanca in Spain, took its roots from Africa—Timbuktu in present-day Mali. So let's get serious with high-quality education in the continent that will help move our continent forward so that we can re-usher ourselves in the world stage. W. J. Perry acknowledged that the Egyptians excelled in all more than other ancient people with their mastery over materials of the most diverse sorts.

These genius attributes of the early Africans can be revisited if we begin to develop quality-oriented education in our various nation states. Let's look forward to better days for the continent of Africa, where the West will begin to count on the Moors like it was in centuries past, when men were men in Africa and we dealt with the West on an equal footing, with them consulting Africans as partners and not as their stooges or puppets.

The need for political changes in the right direction for the benefit of the civil society of Africa cannot be delayed anymore. Also, the issues of serious infrastructure development, conflict resolution, and early intervention in war-torn areas can no longer depend on the West to initiate. Rather, Africans themselves should take the initiative to intervene. This will make us stand on our feet like other regions of world. The ideas of Kwame Nkrumah of Ghana in forming the Organisation of African Unity (OAU) should be reinvigorated in all conscious African minds.

CHAPTER 1

Education

We can say that 'education' in its narrow technical sense means a formative process by which society deliberately teaches its accumulated knowledge, customs, values, and skills from one generation to another, such as with instructions in schools. Some jurisdictions have been created and have recognised the right to education since 1952. Article 2 of the first protocol to the European Convention on Human Rights obliges all signatories to guarantee the rights to education. In all global levels, the United Nations' international convention on economic, social, and culture rights of 1966 guarantees this right under Article 13.

It can also be said that education means a way through which the aims and habits of a group of people live on from one generation to the next. It also means 'train', as is indicated in the Latin word *educatio*. It means to train someone to change his thinking, feelings, etc.

Can you imagine being unable to read the words on this page? What if you couldn't speak your country's official language? Suppose you were unable to point to your homeland on a map of the world. Countless children in the world will grow up in this circumstance.

The continent of Africa will remain in this very situation if we don't do anything fast to move forward. What about your child? Should your child go to school to acquire education?

In many countries around the world, primary and secondary education is compulsory and free for every child till the age of 18 years.

However, in Africa, the reverse is the case. The Convention on the Rights of the Child considers formal education to be a fundamental right, and so does the Universal Declaration of Human Rights.

In some countries, though, education might not be free and might be a financial burden to parents. Let us look at this matter through the eyes or perspective of many parents who want their children to be literate either through formal or religious education. Just like George W. Bush, the one-time president of the United States of America, said, 'Leave no child behind.' This was an act he pursued during his term as president, seeing the importance of education in American society. Regardless of the high literacy rate in the United States, the president believed that children have that fundamental right to education.

In many nations of the African continent, this has not been the case, even in the twenty-first century's high-tech world. So many children have not only been left behind, but they have also been completely denied the right or opportunity to an education. This is not only by their own parents and guardians, but also due to poverty or financial constraints and state policies.

Education is paramount in the life of a person, particularly children. If a child is not able to read and write, it will deprive him or her of much vital information to function in a given environment. For example, individuals with an education become informed and better at understanding others and have broader and more open minds to accommodate and tolerate people with different opinions. The need to educate the children of Africa is pertinent to its sociopolitical, industrial, and technological advancement. This is what the continent needs to move forward. The No Child Left Behind Act of President George W. Bush shows how this issue is important. Not minding the literacy rate in the United States, the government still finds it important to educate more children as well as adults who happened to miss the chance as children to acquire it.

The educational systems around the world vary in nature—preschools; primary, secondary, or tertiary schools; vocational schools; universities; or alternative education. The continent of Africa needs to invest in those systems for upward movement and development so that its people can compete in the global world of today and the future.

There have been in existence many systems of education. We need only to pick the ones that suit our nations and implement them fully to empower our people.

Systems of Education/Schooling

Schooling/educational systems involve institutionalised teaching and learning in relation to a curriculum, which itself is established according to a predetermined purpose of the schools in the system. You may ask, 'What is the purpose of education or schooling?' Education or schooling helps us to develop reasoning about persistent questions, master the methods of scientific enquiry, cultivate intellect, and create positive change agents. The purposes and goals of schools are to teach people how to think.

The word 'curriculum' means a set or list of academic disciplines. In formal education, a curriculum includes the lists of courses and their content offered at a school or university. As an idea, 'curriculum' stems from the Latin word for 'racecourse', referring to the course of ideals and experience through which children grow to become adults. It is prescriptive and based on a more general syllabus that merely specifies what topics must be understood and what level to achieve a particular grade or standard.

What does 'discipline' mean in terms of education or school? It is a branch of knowledge that is formally taught at the university or through some other method. Each discipline usually has several subdisciplines and distinguishing lines. Examples of disciplines include natural science, computer science, mathematics, humanities, and social sciences.

Education and schooling vary from formal to alternative education as well as indigenous education. However, all education is important in transforming the society in which we live since through it we train and nurture one generation to the next. So how did education come into existence?

Brief History of Education

According to Professor Dieter of the Freie University of Berlin in 1994, 'Education began either millions of years ago or at the end of 1770. As a science, education cannot be separated from the educational traditions that existed before. Adults trained the young of their society in the knowledge and skills they would need to master, and eventually, it passed on. The evolution of culture and human beings as a species depends on this practice of transmitting knowledge.'

In oral-literate societies, education was achieved through the spoken word. Storytelling continued from one generation to the next, as was the case in the early African continent. Oral language developed into written symbols and letters. Later cultures began to extend their knowledge beyond the basic skills of communicating, trading, gathering food, and practising religion, for example. Formal education and schooling eventually followed. Schooling in this sense was already in place in Africa (Egypt) between 3000 and 500 BC.

The continent had been part of an early educated society. So it is sad that Africa is lacking in all forms of education in the twenty-first century. This brings the idea of making some certain level of education compulsory in the continent of Africa as well as in many nations around the world.

According to UNESCO, due to population growth and the proliferation of compulsory education, in the next thirty years, more people will receive formal education than in all of human history. In this case, the questions are as follows: What is the position of the nations in the continent of Africa in this projection? Are our respective nation states in the continent doing something to see that they will be counted amongst those who have reached this goal, or will they still lag behind as they have over fifty years of independence?

The Education We Need

The continent of Africa and its states need all approved and known systems of education for us to move forward in achieving advancements in development, technology, agriculture, economics, and sociopolitical greatness. There have been established systems of education that we have adopted that need to be implemented so that they can function effectively for the benefit of all children in Africa. These systems might include preschools; primary, secondary, and tertiary schools; vocational schools; universities; and alternative education. In fact, many nations already have these in existence, but questions remain regarding the effectiveness in implementation and maintaining the status quo. It is only by quality education that the continent of Africa can emerge from poverty and its backwardness in terms of development. One of the major ways forward is *education*, *education*, and *education* because it enlightens the mind and empowers people for upward movement. Let us have a look at the different types of education or schooling systems that many need or have had opportunities to have. The system of education begins with preschooling.

Preschool Education

This is the education that can give a child the edge in a competitive world and educational climate. During this period of education, children receive the fundamentals; but those who unfortunately do not get this early education will be taught the alphabet, counting, shapes, colours, and designs when they begin their formal education. They will not be behind the children who already possess that knowledge. This system of preschooling is highly required in the African system of education, though some children passed through this system. But the problem here is that it is only for the privileged few who can afford it. However, preschool must be instituted in our education system for all children to benefit from. After preschool comes primary education, which is essential in everyone's life.

Primary Education

This level of education consists of the first five to seven years of formal structured education. This system varies amongst and within countries, but with the same aim. Quality education, which in general consists of six or eight years of schooling, starts at the age of 6. In the global scale, around 89 per cent of primary-age children are enrolled in primary education, and this percentage is rising. Under UNESCO programmes, most countries have committed themselves to achieve universal enrolment in primary education by 2015. In fact, UNESCO projection was not likely met by 2015, which has come and gone. I still remember when about twenty years ago or more, it was said that education will be for all in the year 2000, but that never happened. African nations need compulsory primary education as well as preschool education to empower our children and prepare them for the future.

Schools that provide primary education are called primary schools, and African nations need to invest in this system of education and follow-up education programmes.

Secondary Education

This type of education or schooling is the follow-up after primary education, which is needed to prepare a child for higher education or vocational education, where he or she can acquire skills.

In contemporary educational systems of the world, secondary education comprises the formal education that occurs during adolescence. It is characterised by a transition from the typically compulsory comprehensive primary education, where it exists like in the West for minors, to optional selective tertiary, 'postsecondary', or 'higher' education (e.g. university or vocational school) for adults.

The secondary education system did not emerge in the United states until 1910 because of the rise in the big businesses and technological advancements in factories (e.g. the emergence of electrification) that required skilled workers. The emergence of new challenges creates room for new ways and ideas of doing things. In order to meet new job demands in the United States and other developed countries, high schools were created, and the curriculum focused on practical job skills that would better prepare students for white-collar or skilled blue-collar work. This proved to be beneficial for both the employer and the employee because this improvement to human capital caused employees to become more efficient, which lowered costs for the employer, and skilled employees received a higher pay than employees with just primary educational attainment.

The continent of Africa needs to invest in these types of education to produce people who are skilled to compete in the international market. Most countries in the continent are just churning out students and graduates who lack the required skills in the new technological world we live in. The government needs to invest to improve the existing schools and education programmes to match the standards in the developed countries. Africa has a lot of potential in terms of resources, and we can't continue to depend on the West to manage resources for us. It is in this area that we need to move forward as a continent in particular to be able to move with other continents to be on equal footing with them in terms of advancements in science and technology.

Our human capital needs to be competent enough to work independently in harnessing our resources so that the idea of always waiting on the West and China will be a thing of the past.

Indigenous Education

This refers to the inclusion of indigenous knowledge, methods, and content within formal and nonformal educational systems. In a postcolonial context, the growing recognition and use of indigenous education methods can often be a response to the erosion and loss of indigenous knowledge and language through the processes of colonialism. Also, it can enable indigenous communities to 'reclaim and revalue their languages and cultures and, in so doing, improve the educational success of native students'. This system of education may be needed in areas where formal education has not gained ground or where there is the compulsory idea of letting every child have the opportunity to receive basic education.

Alternative Education

It is known also as nontraditional education since it is used to refer to all forms of education outside of traditional education (for all age groups and levels of education). In one way, it involves not only forms of education designed for students with special needs (ranging from teenage pregnancy to intellectual disability), but also forms of education designed for a general audience and employing alternative educational philosophies and methods.

This type of education differs from traditional compulsory education and is mainly used to improve the lives of the handicapped or those who were unable to get formal education at an early stage in life. We really need to invest in this type of education to help and empower the handicapped in African society. Looking at the West, like the Netherlands, almost all their handicapped citizens are productive in many ways. They acquire either formal or alternative education, which makes them less dependent on family or the government. With their education, they get employed in different fields and make a lot of contribution in the society where they live. But in the continent of Africa, many disabled people have no opportunity to acquire education of any type, and this makes them look like a burden to society and their immediate families. Therefore, let us implement a policy that can empower this group of people through education. This group of people can also be highly productive in the quest of moving the continent forward.

Higher Education

Higher education can be seen as tertiary, third-stage, or postsecondary education. It is also a noncompulsory education level that follows the completion of a school providing secondary education such as high school or secondary school. On the other hand, tertiary education normally includes undergraduate and postgraduate education as well as vocational education. The training colleges and universities are main institutions that provide tertiary education. After tertiary education, students acquire certificates, diplomas, and academic digress (e.g. OND, HND, TTC certificates; BSC and BA degrees).

In most developed nations, a high proportion of the population (up to 50 per cent) have now entered higher education at some time in their lives. This type of education is very important to national economies, both as a significant industry in its own right and as a source of trained and educated personnel for the rest of the economy.

Through higher education, countries produce men and women who go into research and development in many fields—teachers, lawyers, doctors, nurses, engineers, and other professionals who are needed in national development and advancement. In this context, African nations need manpower in the industrial sectors so that they can harness their natural resources and have managers who look after these resources for the benefit of her citizenry. The times of depending on the West and China to come and manage our resources and entire economy have to come to an end. If Africa has to move forward, she has to really invest in these types of education in order to produce highly qualified graduates and technicians to take care of our national demand for technological development and advancement in every sector of our economy.

Adult Education

There is a saying that it is never too late to learn; as long as we live, we learn new things and ideas every day. So if an adult is determined to learn, he or she can make up for his or her lost opportunity as a child through adult education.

This educational programme has become common in many nations around the world. It takes on many forms, ranging from formal class-based learning to self-directed learning to recently e-learning with the advent of the Internet. A number of career-specific courses—such as medical billing and coding, veterinary assistance, real estate licensing, bookkeeping, and many more—are now available to students through the Internet. Also, those who never had chance to be literate now have the opportunity to do so through adult education. This helps to improve the quality of lives in the society we live, such as in the areas of hygiene and environmental upkeep.

It is not only adult education that has created an opportunity for people through education to improve on their well-being. If we look at education in general, we can agree that it has a lot of benefits for the society and in all aspects of life.

Importance of Education

On a global and general scale, education is paramount in national development. In the context of the continent of Africa in particular and other emerging nations in general, it is education that will turn the lives of their citizens around and gears them towards a better future. The importance of education can never be neglected if Africa has to move forward in order to attain its many potentials.

Many human beings are unable to survive properly without an atom of education. Education makes one use his or her potentials to the maximum. It helps men to know how to think, work properly, and make decisions. In short, education increases one's mental state.

Education gives one an identity that separates him in outstanding ways from those who are unable to obtain it. It is important in our lives as a basic need like food, clothes, and shelter. With education, we learn how to interact with others and how to make friends. It gives you the opportunity to be literate even in the smallest level possible, at least to be able to read and write; in fact, it empowers you in many things in life.

Through education, we learn how to control feelings and emotions; it also teaches us how to act in different situations. We all know that education is broad—it does not only teach physics, geography, chemistry, mathematics, history, literature, etc. In fact, it encompasses a lot of things beyond the ordinary curriculum—that is to say, courses. It is said that 'travelling is a part of education' since you can observe and interact with other people and cultures. Many have become well informed of many life issues through travelling from place to place.

In terms of technology, industry, commerce, economics, and politics, education is the motor or engine that drives all these aspects of human society. Education enlightens people's minds and gives them new skills and helps them to adapt. It was the educated elites in Europe that began campaigns into liberalising the Western societies so that they would be able to accommodate foreigners, mostly races other than white. It was the action of educated European liberals that diminished the wicked influence of divisive religion in the West in places like France, Netherlands and Germany.

It was also the power of education that engineered African students in the West to learn about human rights laws and politics, which pushed them to campaign and struggle for the independence of African countries from the European colonial masters. The elite Africans employed education to fight for freedom against oppression, though some of them later turned around and used the same educational ideas to dominate and oppress their own. However, granted it has been applied the wrong way to the detriment of the continent of Africa, it is still better to acquire education than to be illiterates. The lack of it in many of the children has derailed the ability of the continent to move forward.

The power of educational influence on the people both politically and otherwise can never be jettisoned. During 1966, crises in universities were interlinked most of the time. For instance, the problem in the Argentina university spilt to Brazil, just as the education problem in Rhodesia of Ian Smith (now Zimbabwe) spilt over to English universities. Many times, students' rebellions or protests have lead to political changes that have changed lives all around the world.

During the early 1960s, technical education was aimed at providing a properly balanced and well-trained workforce for the development of economic resources in order to promote prosperity of the people. This was the idea according to Paul Hasluck, the then Australian minister of external affairs. The same is true today that African nations need to embrace this idea in order to foster a better tomorrow for their people. Unlike years ago, an illiterate in the world today has limited chances since modern life is based more on the power of Internet and other new technology. In this context, Africa cannot afford to remain where she is without improving and increasing the number of literates through education. There are various tools available today to give those who were unable to obtain education at an early stage in life the chance to do so.

The advent of information and computer technologies (ICT) are set of tools and resources used to communicate, disseminate, create, store, and manage information. Some of these technologies include televisions, computers, radios, the Internet, and telephones. These are made use of to educate people both in formal and informal settings in open and distance education. Pictures and illustrations drive points home better to the less educated in the process of learning.

The use of these technologies is highly needed in a society like ours to make education easier and accessible for both the literate and illiterate. The issues of education and technology have an economic importance in developing nations such as those in Africa in particular. In fact, it has been argued that high rates of education are essential for countries to be able to achieve high levels of economic growth. Some analyses indicate that poor countries should grow faster than rich countries because they can adopt cutting-edge technologies already tried and tested by rich countries. However, technology transfer requires knowledgeable managers, engineers, and technicians who are able to operate new machines or production practices borrowed from the leader in order to close the gap through imitation. In this case, a country's ability to learn from the leader is the function of its stock, 'human capacity'.

The work of Jacob Mincer shows how learning and schooling and human capital of the individual are related. This work has motivated a lot of studies and some controversies. The controversies revolve around how to interpret the impact of schooling. (See Samuel Bowles and Herbert Gintis's argument of 1976 on American schooling.)

The importance of education is so great that only a few points cannot explain it all. Some other reasons for the importance of education include health, social, and moral values as well as personality development. The International Statistical Institute research centre in Voorburg in the Netherlands confirms that over two decades of available information from developing countries show that material education has had an impact on the children's mortality rates. Mothers' values on health matter, and the use of health services has improved saving lives during birth and has reduced mortality rates. Also, a study involving infant mortality in the Republic of Benin in West Africa indicates that illiterate mothers as a group lose children under the age of 5 years at the rate of 167 per 1,000, whereas women with secondary education lost 38.

UNICEF concludes that the level of education is hence a determining factor in infant mortality rate in Benin as it is all over the world. So this is an example of how educating daughters and women in general has benefits. The state as well as parents should take the responsibility of providing a child with basic education.

Education helps in promoting social order in society and develops a world-class workforce. It is also a well-known fact that education teaches moral values and helps to develop a person's personality. Education also improves general thinking.

A society with a great number of literate minds can expand and develop rapidly. So the African continent needs and deserves to invest in educating its citizenry as an avenue to lift the continent out of misery.

CHAPTER 2

Shedding Away the Colonial Influence

The effects of the colonial activities in the continent of Africa are both positive and negative. The continent, therefore, needs to shed away the negative influences of the colonial masters and their 'democrazy', as Fela Kuti of Nigeria calls it instead of the 'democracy' the West is said to have brought to the continent.

Before the advent of the white man, there has been an established system of administration that is democratic in nature in the context of African culture. The existence of the traditional kings, village chiefs, Nzes, Ozo elders, and other age grades was purely democratic in nature. There were rules of law, separation of powers, and delegated legislation in place. These structures were highly respected, obeyed, and honoured by her citizenry. However, when the white man came with democracy, she introduced the divide-and-rule system, a dictatorship mentality, and a militant attitude, employing force to compel their subjects to obey or die. This attitude still exists in every political or democratic setting in the African continent today. Those who rule do so with the mentality of brutal force of domination and control of the lives of the common citizens without regards to human rights and people's rights as citizens of a given state.

Many political leaders raised and nurtured by the West who introduced a system of democracy were tutored to dominate their subjects, as that was the attitude of the white man when they were in control of their respective colonies. The after-effects of this mentality and culture linger on in the continent's political and democratic system. The rulers have no say on the state of affairs of the land; rather, the rulers control and dictate the life pattern of their subjects. Most of the time, there is a possibility to seek redress in terms of legality.

The politics of domination created by the West in terms of their own style of democracy destroyed the established democratic structure in the African continent then. The king of the Ashanti in 1817 and before then had been governing his subjects democratically without many problems till the white man brought his own type of democracy, which then produced problems in the Ashanti empire. Since the West needed the policy of domination to control her new subjects, she decided to hand-pick rulers and taught them how to use the policy of intimidation and domination to rule the people. When their masters left Africa in their hands, the groomed leaders applied this system to the detriment of the entire continent. Minority tribes were chosen as favourites by the West to dominate majority tribes—an idea that was not in existence before the advent of Western colonialism. This ushered in long-raging violence and conflict in Africa. This has continued since the West left the shores of Africa in terms of giving Africa political independence without economic independence. However, in the real sense of things, Africa is not partially independent since the West continues to interfere in who runs the affairs of different African nations. If the choice of the people doesn't suit the interest of the West, the people's choice is nullified.

Many stories abound in the continent where those with a nationalist agenda for Africa are removed from power with the use of brutal force in terms of an aided inside military coup d'état to unseat anti-West leaders (e.g. Patrice Lumumba of Congo, Murtala Mohammed of Nigeria, Thomas Sankara of Burkina Faso, Kwame Nkrumah of Ghana, and Tunde Idiagbon of Nigeria). The idea of domination, intimidation, and training given to the trained leaders has dominated our political climate of the so-called democracy that the West left behind instead of what we knew in our own old setting of democratic ruling. This appalling system of democracy left for us by the West has to be re-examined and possibly modified to suit our own setting. This approach would be for the benefit of the continent and her citizenry.

Building Confidence

Africans have to learn and know who they are before the advent of the West in the continent. When you know who you are, you have confidence in whatever you are doing. If we begin to recover, then we can rediscover ourselves. The mentality that you are black and know nothing has to be jettisoned from the minds of Africans if we really want to make headway in our development. Africans should look back in Africa's history when her people were great warriors, inventors, wrestlers, quality farmers, and the inventors of first sailing ship. They did mummification, built pyramids, and were descendants of Imhotep, the father of medicine, amongst other things. They built the great centre of learning in Timbuktu (now Mali), from which the first University of Salamanca in Spain took root.

We should remember the days when we were called the Moors and not blacks or Negroes, the time when the white man consulted Africans as friends and not when they began to call us blacks or Negroes, and the days when Europeans invited African leaders as those they respected and treated with dignity. We have to understand that there was a time when the West came to Africa to obtain food to feed her citizens and not when she began to feed Africans. We should gain the confidence that there were times in the past when our streets were decorated with trees and not littered with dirt. Africans should have the confidence to learn and tell their own story of the mass nature of the continent and not leaving it in the hands of the whites, the majority of whom don't even know that Africa is a continent. Rather, most Westerners still see and refer to Africa as a state or nation, just like France or Italy.

In fact, one Greek American who lived in New York City while working with me at Thetford in Etten-Leur in the Netherlands in 2011 asked me what the capital of Africa was. In all honesty, I told him 'Athens' since he was foolish enough to see Africa as Greece, not as a continent. You know what they say—if someone asks you a foolish question, you give him or her a foolish answer. Some of them do not know that only the Democratic Republic of the Congo is as big as all of Europe or, say, France, Spain, Italy, and England put together.

Your confidence as an African should come from the fact that there was a time when honest Europeans acknowledged the richness of Africa, the ability of Africans to weave their own clothes, and their ability to carry out trade even in kola nuts, which the Arabs then used to call 'the coffee of Negroes'. Though some Eurocentric critics of Africa always say we talk of the past achievements of Africa, but what of present achievements? However, we've been lost in the present because of their imperialistic influence, which limits us or makes us feel like we aren't good enough to recover from our old ability to invent. Anyway, there were some honest European witnesses that attested to the ability of Africans to be productive, organised, and democratic in nature. I will not hesitate to draw your attention to some of them and their honest attestations.

For instance, W. W. Reade wrote in *The Martyrdom of Man* in 1872 that two of his colleagues told him that they 'were astonished to find among the Negroes magnificent courts; regiments of cavalry; the horses caparisoned in silk for gala days and clad in coats of mail for war; long trains of camels laden with salt, corn, and cloth and cowries shells (which form the currency) and kola nuts which the Arabs call the "the Coffee of the Negroes"'. There were also European merchants and travellers who were unbiased on their accounts on Africa's civilisation of the Guinea coast days. Filippo Pigafetta's *Relatione del reame del Congo*, which was published in 1591, stated that the circumference of the kingdom was 1,695 miles divided into six administrative provinces. He went further to explain that the people were 'a swarming crowd dressed in silk and velvet, well-ordered, and down to the most minute details, powerful rulers, flourishing industries, civilized to the marrow of their bones'.

In the same then Guinea coast of Africa, the European captains 'were astonished to find streets well cared for, bordered for several leagues in length by two rows of trees; for many days they passed through a country of magnificent fields, a country inhabited by men clad in brilliant costumes, the stuff of which they had woven themselves!' (See page 16 of *New African* magazine, 2008.)

Another honest European also attested to the respect of Africans in his defence to the prejudice against Africans. In 1772, a certain Samuel Estwick wrote a memorandum to the Right Honourable Lord Mansfield with regards to a court case. 'In general they (blacks) are void of genius, and seem almost incapable of making any progress in civility or science . . . They seem unable to combine ideas, or to pursue a chain of reasoning . . .' However, James Ramsay refuted him, saying, 'As far as I can judge, there is no difference between the intellects of whites and blacks, but such as circumstances and education naturally produce' (See *New African* magazine, October 2008. Extracts are from Akinyi von K'Orinda-Yimbo's *Darkest Europe and Africa's Nightmare*). Anyway, how I wish that Estwick is alive to see the achievements of people like Philip Emeagwali and a host of other great Africans.

Also, Thomas Jefferson, the first secretary of state of the United States who became the third president of the USA in March 1801, in his own book in 1785, *Notes on the State of Virginia*, said, 'Comparing them [Negroes] by their faculties of memory, reason and imagination, it appears to me, that in memory they are equal to the whites; in reason much more inferior, as I think one could scarcely be found capable of tracing and comprehending the investigations of Euclid; and that in imagination, they are dull, tasteless, and anomalous.' In fact, he forgot that Euclid, the world's greatest mathematician, was an African. It is also doubtful if Jefferson himself was not black since he never spoke of his mother throughout his lifetime. He was described as someone with corky skin, and he mentioned of having being carried at the back of a Negro woman. So he was possibly black. (See the history of the American presidents in https://www.loc.gov.)

Your confidence should stem from the fact that even today, the Europeans don't accord you respect as an African, but there were days when they recognised the potentials we had and benefited from it. And due to their greedy and jealousy, they have relegated us.

In the beginning of thirteenth century, a certain Wolfram von Eschenbach of Germany created the image of the so-called noble Moor as a knight full of virtue, courage, and a ripe fruit of faithfulness. With such famous institutions of learning like Timbuktu, the Moors' education was touted to be beyond any other; he was pure and brave in battle too. No other knight before him was so gentle, for he knew no injustice, as Von Eschenbach described him.

Today, the Dutch (of the Netherlands) describe Africans as '*langzaam*'. In English, it means 'slow'; but they forgot that their forefathers came to Africa to take Africans to fight for them in Indonesia, where they were unable to fight to maintain their grip on the land that did not belong to them. The black Dutchmen, as they used to call them, form a bulk of the Java population in Indonesia today. However, because of their racist European mentality, they see us as being slow people today. Because of this, after 1945, they went to Turkey and Morocco to bring workers to enjoy the sweat of Africans. They can deny it, but if you know your history, it can give you confidence that what they say you are today is not what you really are.

The honest European historians know the truth, and some acknowledge it without prejudice. This group of honest Europeans are needed to educate their sons and daughters whose minds are filled with prejudices and untrue stories about Africa's present and past state of things.

Members of the European media, past and present, have been the agents of discrimination and racism towards Africans in peddling uncensored stories about the black man. We need to know our history and the courage and bravery of our ancestors who were even referred to with great respect as Allah's black ravens. Black Africans were part of the army that defeated North Africa and crossed the Strait of Gibraltar to conquer Spain in the seventh century (*New African* magazine, October 2008).

Renouncing the Christian and Muslim Ideas of the Imperialist

Africans (Moors) or blacks, as the colonial and Arab hegemony later called us because of their greedy and imperialist inclination, had their own religion before the advent of Christian West and Muslim Arabs. These two dominating religions in Africa have been a source of a major damage to African culture and the tradition of its people. They have served as a rallying point of violent conflict and division amongst the Africans (blacks) and Africans in diaspora. It has in one way or the other blinded our people and has served as opium for the masses. It kept us quiet as an excellent stuff so that the West and Arab expansionists/imperialists could cart away our resources. It was well functional in Africa and other places before the white man set his foot in Africa with his religion, which became opium and a way to keep us quiet, as Napoleon Bonaparte and Karl Marx described it in 1797 and 1894, respectively.

These two foreign religions brought division amongst Africans and still do today. For instance, a Muslim person from Somalia, Nigeria, Sierra Leone, or any other country in Africa prefers to align himself or herself with Muslims from other continents than his or her fellow Africans who are not Muslims. In the West, the so-called black (African) Muslims have mostly become brainwashed with the theology of Islam. This makes them not stick to their kind; rather, they are foolishly inclined to a foreign religion. No matter how hard you try to educate or open their minds to the realities, they will never accept them or learn. This has created a disparity amongst Africans that is one of blood and colour since the whites tend to stick to their kind despite their religious affiliation.

Many of these black Africans tend to imbibe Arab culture instead of African culture, thinking that Arab culture is Islamic culture. This attitude has to change in order to help Africa move forward. They need to embrace brotherhood rather than unfounded attachment to religion of the slave masters. An Arab adage says 'Me and my brother against my cousin, and me and my cousin against an outsider'. Let's be wise and renew and transform our minds to the betterment of Africa and her descendants—that is, those who are willing to accept that they are Africans. Remember Peter Tosh said, 'No matter where you find yourself, if you are black, you are African.' Despite how toned your skin may be or how far you want to align yourself with whites, you will still be seen as being black. Half-white and half-black (mixed-race) children are always classified as black by the Eurocentrics; that is a lesson for you.

In fact, before the advent of the two divisive ideas of the newly formed religions, Africans had their own type of religion and lived in peace without any problem. Even in the Bible, there is the story of the Ethiopian eunuchs who were baptised by Philip. So blacks had contact with Christianity before they started to sell it to us in a different manner, with its hidden intention to loot (Acts 8: 26). Just like the late Chinua Achebe said, 'They told us to close our eyes so that we can pray. Before we opened our eyes, our lands were in their hands.'

These two foreign religions have devastated the continent of Africa and its citizenry in many ways—politically, economically, socially, educationally, and otherwise. Islam in Africa has limited socioeconomic development and educational development in the sense that it limits women from obtaining quality education. This hampers mental development, which is needed in political, economic, and technological development as well as innovation. The religion of Islam does not welcome the participation of women in some of these activities and therefore applies a lot of rules to hinder Islamic women from participation.

Christian religion in a way has its own guilt in this also, though not as serious as Islam, in the sense that it has become, like what Marx said, 'opium', which disorients some of Africa's young men and women. Instead of them using their time to produce goods and services, they would rather tend to spend their days in churches day and night, shouting and clapping. They fail to understand that God encouraged management and productivity. It is written in the Bible that 'a hand that doesn't work should not eat as well (2 Thessalonians 3: 8–11). But this doesn't only mean physical labour; it also includes God's work of spreading the message. Remember Paul worked to provide for himself. Some have become brainwashed with the white man's religion of Christianity; in the West, it is no more so dearly cherished. The purpose then was to sell to the Africans to pacify them and make them quiet so that their resources could easily be obtained. Many Christian churches around Europe have been turned to mosques or discotheque halls because of the lack of congregations. However, I am not saying here that you should abandon Jehovah, but I suggest you look back to the method and type of early African religion and how they worshiped God; that might make our lives better.

Remember, brethren, that there were times of the Oriental Moors or the cultured Ethiopians who had dark skin but had represented a culture more superior to that of the Europeans. Since Christ came from their corner of the world, they have embraced Christianity at a time when the religion was struggling to take root in Greece and Rome. The African blacks that the European Christians presented to their people as uncivilised had been richly clothed and bejewelled as well as well educated and cultured in conduct. (See extracts of Akinyi von K'Orinda-Yimbo's work in the *New African* magazine, 8 October 2008). Armed, the Moors or Ethiopians had threatened the Europeans on their ancestral land. The initial contact or interaction between Europeans and Africans had been initiated by Africans coming to Europe and not the other way round.

However, when the Europeans started to compete with one another to possess our land on the Guinea coast of Africa, they came in contact with a new breed of Africans who they thought were inferior to them both economically and spiritually. This motivated them to look down on us due to their inward prejudice and thereby forget the achievements of Muslims and Coptic Christians of Africa, whom they once admired. Before the Western Christian type of religion and Arab Muslim expansionism in Africa, the African traditional religion as well as the Coptic Christian religion had no conflict that threatened African society or the African continent.

Then entered the Arab Muslims between AD 639 and 708 with their conflict- and war-oriented attitude, which has persisted to date in Africa. In fact, before this time, all of Africa—the North included—had no African ancestry. All the pyramids and monuments were the works of continental Africans. For instance, Pharaoh Djoser, ruling in the third dynasty between 5018 and 4989 BC, was black. Today, our history, both in terms of religion and other achievements, has been swept under the rug by European writers and some historians. (See extracts of Akinyi von K'Orinda-Yimbo's work in the *New African* magazine, October 2008).

When we look at the Ahiara Declaration (1969), Biafra only would have been the 'none colonized black nation'. You can see the depth of Chukwuemeka 'Emeka' Odumegwu-Ojukwu's hatred for the effects of the religion of Islam on the continent of Africa: 'Because we refused as black people to accept the contagion of Islam and its militant Arabism, we were hated by some Arab Muslim nations then.' This gave them the opportunity to support and aid the Nigerian government to commit genocide against Biafra and her children.

In fact, the Christian Protestant English were part of the conspiracy to massacre and commit genocide against Biafra. The same is true today in Sudan, where the Arab Muslims have been committing genocide against the black people of Sudan. Most of the raging wars that have ravaged and derailed the African continent have been supported or aided by the religion of Islam or Christianity in conjunction with afflicted governments around the globe. In fact, in Mali, Nigeria, Mauritania, Sudan, Chad, Congo, Somalia, Kenya, and others, conflict has in one way or another a religious dimension. These two foreign religions have to be analysed and reshaped to suit

African culture so that we can move forward in a progressive manner rather than allow them to continue to ruin our future and that of our children, if they have not already done so. However, I still believe that if we discover now, we can then recover for a better tomorrow for Africa.

When China and Russia avoided these two religions, they were able to make progress. Anyway, I am not trying to sound antireligion here, but I am suggesting that we take these religions in a different way, where they don't hinder our development anymore. God himself created us all and empowered us to produce and manage our resources, but we left that duty in the hands of others while we were chasing religion around.

W. J. Perry in his book *The Growth of Civilization* made us to understand that the earlier people, just like ancient Africans, were peaceful. The religions of Islam and European Christianity forced on Africans brought with them unending conflict and violence in the continent, which refuse to come to an end. In fact, the violent effects of these two religions have continued to promote disunity in Africa. All these religious conflicts and violent causes and effects have been used to aid the enslavement of Africans in many forms. Our citizens were carted away as slaves and traded as commodities by the European Arab imperialists. So let us do away with this colonial influence as much as we can so that we will be able to reunite as a people.

As Africans, do not forget that both religions of Christianity and Islam have a discriminatory attitude against black people of Africa and their descendants. As far back as 1857, during the colonial days, many educated Africans were not valued or regarded by the Europeans even though they said they were their brothers and sisters in Christ. There was this joke that went with the statement by an American president that 'all men are born equal', but they always say, 'But you know what we mean.' That played in European colonial Christian masters when it comes to the Bible, which indicates that we are equal before God. They treated Africans with disrespect, not minding their open declaration in the churches that we are brothers and sisters in Christ.

By the time the European colonialists took over Central Africa, some groups of African Christians pushed to start their own independent church in the British colony of Nyasaland (now Malawi). Elliot Kamwana in 1908 started the Watch Tower sect (Jehovah's

Witnesses). He preached the second coming of Christ Jesus on earth and said that he will free Africans from their European oppressors. The British Christian authorities were at odds with his message, and they got him arrested.

But Kamwana's Watch Tower movement spread to neighbouring lands, such as Rhodesia (now Zimbabwe), where the movement brought weighed unrest to the white colonialists, which shortened their rule there.

The same was true about a Congolese preacher by the name of Simon Kimbangu, who said that God was coming to liberate the Congolese from the oppressive colonial government of Belgium. During 1921, he claimed to be godsent for his people to free them from the oppressors, and he was believed by his people. He was arrested and imprisoned for preaching the same freedom message and salvation the European Christian colonialists preached to us in order to take our resources. In Christ's message, they were prejudicial to it, seeing themselves as only God's elect, whose sole authority was to preach the Good News.

In fact, I wish all Africans would come to see reason, think, and embrace the African traditional religion or practise the two imperialist religions of Islam and Christianity in a way that will allow for unity and not be divisive, the way the imperialists made it to be. The unity and blood relationship of all blacks/Africans and diaspora should be more important to us than the religious affliction that is destroying us and hampering our development.

CHAPTER 3

Establishing and Maintaining Effective Institutions

The African nation states can have a rapid upward movement in terms of development and innovations when they begin to establish and learn more about how to maintain existing institutions that they already have. We have to learn how to shake off the imperialistic attitude of institutions created and managed with the attitude of inequality. Our thinking should be directed in line with our ancient heritage. We should think of the challenges of today and the changes of the future. Many parts of the world today have emerged from the ills or negative effects of colonialism; we are still being held hostage by this factor. Reformation and a rebranding attitude are what we need to move Africa forward individually as states and collectively as a continent.

Our doctors, teachers, nurses, technologists, scientists, pharmacists, police, judges, and military should work effectively together to respond to the demands of our people with brilliant inventions, innovations, and new ways of maintaining our existing institutions. Our teachers should learn new ways of teaching to raise quality pupils and students that can compete in world markets. The armed forces and police should see themselves as servants and protectors of the citizens of given nations, not as an oppressive or brutal force against the people as the imperialist raised them. You know when you raise a child with violent behaviour, he or she is likely to carry it over. In fact, the colonial masters raised our forces, both the police and army, with a violent attitude to achieve their aims. And when they left, this attitude has continued on the part of our forces, who harass, intimidate, and even kill us, even in some unprovoked situations. I think that has to do with a copycat of character, as W. J. Perry indicated in his book *The Growth of Civilization* concerning the origin of war: 'Is it true that an infant when in any way thwarted will show anger, and start to make violent attempts to get its own way? May it not be that it is reacting to the recollection of a former experience when, for instance, it had been slapped by an angry mother, or had observed the process in the case of an elder brother or sister?' (1937, page 209).

In case of existing institutions such as the judiciary, public services, and health welfare, there is a need to make these institutions function effectively and perfectly for the benefit of the citizens. This should be of paramount importance, more than its use for the benefits of the few political elites and families. The institution of judiciary should be highly effective to make use of the rule of law. This will eliminate the idea where many in the African continent have grown to become above the law of the states. This hampers a lot of forward movement and hinders democratic structure. The police and armed forces' work become difficult where the institution of judiciary is ineffective in carrying out its function to serve the interest of the people. Health institutions are highly needed to be modernised and equipped with modern technology so that we can face the new diseases emerging every day. In fact, we need to create and maintain effective democratic institutions as other parts of the world are doing. The collaboration amongst African nations cannot be neglected, for that will enable the continent to work jointly in finding solutions to its peculiar problems and not relying and depending on outside powers.

The continent of Africa has come of age where she can stand on her own feet, just like other continents are doing or have done. Asia and the Middle East have emerged from the shackles of imperialistic influence and are competing with the rest of the world in many areas. Though their situations might look different, the whites prefer to align themselves with the yellow race and Arabs than with Africans. They have been partners in crime against the black race in exploiting her and her descendants around the world. When Haiti defeated Napoleon Bonaparte of France and his great army, she was still forced to pay the man she defeated in a war instead of the other way around. In fact, this contributed to the poverty that this nation continues to face to date.

This should make us work even harder in developing ourselves and working closely together to reform and maintain effective institutions to our advantage. Leaders of Africa should reorient their minds to lead us and not to rule since good leaders are for the good and happiness of their citizens. People like Mao Zedong of China, Mahathir Mohamad of Malaysia, and Yoshida Shigeru of Japan led their respective countries to move forward; and they are today enjoying the benefits and resolve of those leaders.

To establish and maintain institutions effectively needs quality educated and disciplined citizenry. Those sent abroad on scholarship to learn should return to help in raising new people with quality skills to benefit the continent. There is great need of people with true nationalist ideas in order to meet these challenges facing us as a continent and as a people. We need patriotism, love, and devotion in the continent of Africa as a whole as well as in the individual nations. Those who work in our respective institutions should have regard and believe in the sanctity of human life and the dignity of the human person.

Some may ask, what the hell is this guy talking about? Do African states or nations lack institutions or managers for these institutions? My answer to these questions is yes with a 'but' in the sense that the only existence doesn't make it perfect. The continent needs functional, quality, honest, and credible managers whose interests are for the nation states and not those with an in-depth corrupt attitude to the detriment of the citizens. Well-maintained institutions and quality managers would have a great positive effect on our economy as individual states as well as a collective effect on the continent. For instance, the introduction of health insurance in Ghana by John Kufuor's government is a welcome development that should be copied by other African countries where it is not in existence. Let us invest in quality and effective institutions that will help us reshape our continent just as other continents are doing or have done.

Further, in this chapter, we are going to look at different institutions that we need to establish or how to effectively maintain existing ones for the betterment of the lives in Africa. In fact, situations have to improve in the continent in areas of building institutions that are effective and efficient, for that is one of the greatest solutions to the inept forward movement of the continent. The lack of strong, effective, and efficient institutions has contributed greatly to corruption and the lack of unity in Africa.

Many countries around the globe that have survived or emerged from the state of poverty have done so through effective and quality institutions. The importance of this has to be paramount in the consciousness of African leaders as well as the citizens themselves. These institutions are discussed below.

Judiciary Institution

The need for a quality, efficient, and effective judiciary system is required in every African nation. Also, the African continent can establish a centre for judiciary training to train those who interpret the law so that they can function in an independent manner where the law will be no respecter of persons.

'Judiciary' can be defined as a system of courts of law for the administration of justice. Its institution can be divided into courts, arbitrary tribunals, and quasi-judiciary. This institution refers to the dynamic judiciary education needed by both federal provinces and territorial judges. This empowers them to manage judiciary issues or matters of a given state. Education is very much needed in this area, which will foster responsible decision-making by officials of the institution without compromising judiciary independence. Judiciary independence improves the rule of law and helps the separation of power to have its proper place in a given nation. When the rule of law and separation of power have their place in this society of ours, the citizenry will always feel the dividends of democracy. Different African nations need this institution and its effectiveness in creating an enabling environment in improving good governance, which will later improve lives in the continent.

One of the most important things that people in the developed nations of the world have enjoyed is the rights of the citizens, which has been maintained through efficient and quality institutions that guarantee these rights. When the judiciary functions the way it should, the citizens of a given state benefit because the rule of law applies. Those who are limited can seek redress in the court of law. When people's rights are denied, the confidence to use civil means to address the issue is there because the judiciary is there to protect them by interpreting what the law demands in their case.

Democracy, they say, is the 'government of the people, by the people, and for the people'. So what maintains this is good operation and respect to the rule of law. Many have won cases against the government or state in nations where the judiciary is completely independent and does not compromise in its functions and discharge from her duty. The judiciary should give people the confidence that they will protect them through the power of the institution. Individuals in a given state can sue the state or a state official in the court of law with confidence that he or she will get justice so long as he or she is right (e.g. *Railroad Stockholders* v. *Young* (state attorney general in the US), *Larson* v. *Domestic and Foreign Commerce Corporation*, 337 US 682 [1949], *Bowoto* v. *Chevron Corporation in Nigeria* [2008], *Gani Fawehinmi* v. *Nigerian Bar Association* [1989], *Wiwa* v. *Royal Dutch Shell* [2009]).

When the judiciary has the power and independence to take these cases against authorities or powerful corporations despite their links to the state, then the people under such a system will be happy and enjoy full rights to seek redress when their rights are infringed on. In fact, this is the type of judiciary that we need in the African continent to move the nation states forward. This is the difference between the developed countries and the developing countries like ours. The lack of independence of the judiciary in most nations of Africa is one of the factors hampering the continent from development and moving forward. The growth of the continent is limited when many government officials and heads of states are immune from prosecution over crimes. The immunity clause enshrined in the laws of many countries has encouraged corruption, violence, and crimes against the citizenry of the nations of Africa.

The judges operate with fear and in favour of those who are in power, while the weak receive excessive sentencing for minor crimes. Those who have no one to speak for them have become the victims of our own type of democracy unlike what is obtainable in a real democratic state, where the judiciary functions in respect to the rule of law. There have been cases in developed nations where the judiciary has been silent for some powerful persons and corporations, but they are only few and in most cases can be revisited to seek real justice. The case is different when it comes to Africa. In fact, more is needed to be done in this factor to improve lives and governance and move the continent forward.

When people fear the law, it gives room for less corruption, unwanted violence, and crimes both by the citizens and those in power. This is because the judiciary is able and willing to interpret the law independently without compromising or being afraid of someone or making some believe that they are above the law.

African nations fought for independence, hence thinking that the rule of law is the foundation of their struggle against imperialism. So the judiciary has to become the most important arm of every given state in the continent. It should be seen as the instrument of protection of the citizens and the defence of their liberties, interpreting the will of the struggle and promoting values of the so-called independence we have. Those who rule and the ones being ruled should bear in mind and respect the judiciary so that citizens will find it possible and easy to have recourse to courts of law when his or her rights or liberties are interfered with or threatened. This will make him or her count on the support of fellow citizens. Those in power should also remember that they will leave power one day and become ordinary citizens, where they will no more escape the arms of the judiciary. Having this in mind will make people fear the law and respect its institutions.

In reality, does the justice process seem remote and far from the life of the ordinary citizen of a given state anywhere and in particular Africa? This is a question each and every one of us in this great continent has to ponder and be part of to obtain the answer by making sure in his or her little office that justice will no more remain remote from his or her fellow citizen. I challenge our respective judiciaries to uphold independence of their offices because it will contribute in lifting and moving our continent forward.

It might not be possible for me to express all the areas that have to be covered in terms of the institution of the judiciary; these include functions, operations, and benefits to the citizens of continent. I appeal to both the ruled and the rulers to bring to mind the importance of this institution in the process of developing the continent. Sometimes to an honest mind, you will ask yourself, why has Africa remained stagnant and not really catching up with other continents in terms of development and moving forward? In fact, the answer isn't far-fetched. Respect the rule of law. Give the judiciary the power to operate independently. If you are an ordinary citizen and are needed to witness, do it for the interest of the independence of the judiciary and not for your own interest or the interest of tribes, clans, or political affiliations.

If you give honest witness where the judiciary functions efficiently and effectively, there might be no threat to your life, for the arms of the law will protect you.

The judiciary should also give such a citizen hope that he or she will be protected by holding to the ethics of the institutions, respecting the rule of law, and discharging his or her duty with respect to the person's status or official capacity. Let's work together to empower and strengthen this institution to the benefit of all, for it will change and improve lives in the continent.

Remember the former president of Egypt and his family are facing the law today; it might possibly be your turn or mine in the future. This has given the Egyptians confidence in their system, and it can be done in your own system if we work together for the common interest of all citizens.

The change we need is in our hands, so let us contribute to make the institution of the judiciary independent and powerful.

The Police Force

The police institution is one of the most essential institutions, very much like the judiciary. It is the responsibility of the police force to bring about the maintaining of law and order and guarding of the security of the people and the nation. The collaboration between the police and the judiciary is highly needed for the rights and safety of the citizens. After a case is reported to the police and an investigation is made, it is the duty of the police to charge or refer the case to court. In this case, during the court hearing, the presiding judge and lawyers on both sides are heard in order for the judge to decide his or her ruling in the case.

The police force, like other institutions of the society and nation states in the continent, needs to be reformed so that it can better fulfil its function in a given nation. The need for highly educated or literate minds is of great significance so that they will be able to understand the importance of their duty to both the ruled and the rulers. In the past, many illiterates have been absorbed in the police and imposed a lot of limitations in discharging their duties in an efficient and effective manner. It is the duty of the government to improve this institution so that they will be of benefit to both the state and the citizens. The members of the police institution have to absorb the new ideals and new social order in the continent of Africa. A lot of criticisms of their poor service quality have been levelled against the police in different African nations by the citizens. They accuse them of intimidation, harassment, corruption, bribery, and inefficiency, which is not far from the truth. Cases abound in Nigeria, Kenya, South Africa, Cameroon, and other nations in Africa where the brutality and abuse against the citizens are captured on video.

These facts cannot be denied by honest people, even some in the police force. However, some of these evils and weaknesses can be traced to the colonial/imperialistic influence in the institution, like many other institutions of our different societies. Today, Africans should remember the early days in places like the Yoruba and Igbo communities of Nigeria, where there were local groups that acted and functioned like the police. This group in Igboland is called Umuokoro Oha, and the one in the Yoruba community is called the Egba. If the chief orders a citizen to appear in the community square to answer questions of misbehaviour or theft and the person in question refuses to honour such an invitation, the local police will go fetch him or her wherever he or she might be or hiding. This was effective and worked for them. They were men of great strength and integrity who discharged their duties in the interest of their respective communities and leaders.

Today, our police should be trained to function for the interest of their citizens and the state, not acting in a disgruntled manner for their selfish interests or those of their tribesmen or their political fathers. For when this becomes the case, as it has been in many years in different nations in the continent since after independence, a copycat of the method of operation under their colonial masters. For Africa to move forward, this type of police institution needs to be transformed so that it can function more like the police force in other developed and democratic nations around the world. Many democracies have survived and are maintained by the effective and efficient functioning of the police and the judiciary. These two institutions of law and order and the prosecution of those who contravene the law have the power to protect the rights of the citizens and make democracy a thing to be cherished by any person.

The progress that is expected in Africa can manifest when our police force embraces and contributes to the ideals of change and progress that we need. The conduct of the police force in the continent must be in the spirit of nationalistic ideals, just like the early nationalists in the continent who fought for independence in the interest of their people, though some of them later became drunk with power, seeing themselves as indispensible. However, they are not around anymore today, which is an indication to others that they can't be around forever. So they have to leave a good legacy for those after them to emulate. Respect must be given to the first president of Botswana, who, after his first time as president, voluntarily left power for others to contribute to the good of the country. The police force in the continent should try to be the people's police—that is to say, a champion for the rights of the people. The policeman is not there only to arrest those who break the law. He should be there to help people avoid doing the wrong thing; from time to time, the police can organise forums where they let the citizens know what they are allowed by the law and what contravenes the law of the land. This will improve the relationship between the police and the people, and many will be able to know their limits when it comes to the law, and this will also make their job easier.

They say the police is your friend, so indeed they should be so that they don't exploit the ignorance of the civil rights of the citizens. On the contrary, it should be or is the duty of the police where such ignorance exists to teach the citizen his or her rights. The reform that is needed in Africa's police force should be around those who have learned and have the good attributes spoken of above—those whose selfless, honest, and patriotic character can't be questioned. These types of minds should take charge of rebuilding the different police forces in the continent so that citizens will feel safe and will be able to see the police as a friend and not as dictators' tool of oppression.

The institution of education should also help in building an efficient and quality police in the sense of organising educational programmes that will help those who have limited education or training. Some police don't function so well because of lack of good education but are devoted to their duty as police and want to perform better for the interest of the citizens and the nation. This group needs access to distance education to improve their academic level. When these institutions collaborate with each other, we can make progress in changing the course of our blessed continent.

It doesn't mean that there is no police corruption, brutality, as well as inefficiency in other developed continents such as Europe, North America, and others; but the difference is that they are limited and that every police officer knows the cost when he or she is caught breaking the law. The judiciary is there to handle and deal with such a police officer. But in the context of many nations in Africa, these police officers and their pot-bellied political leaders are immune from prosecution. The judiciary is ineffective and powerless and has respect for the people instead of the law.

In fact, this hampers progress. When people's lives and properties can't be protected by the institutions of the police and the judiciary, then the citizens are on their own. They become prey to the mercy of the big guys who do what they like since they know that they are above the law of the land. A better and more progressive and innovative Africa is not far if we maintain and reform our institutions.

The Armed Services

The armed forces or military of a nation or nations is defined to include its army, navy, air force, marines, etc. *Collins Dictionary* defines it as above (1991, 1993, 1998, 2000, 2003). It can also be said to be service people in the military such as soldiers, troops, and the infantry.

We all know that the strength or the population of a nation's army can be a measure of the country's or nation's strength or capability compared with that of other nations. The nations with the largest armies may be a threat to others because of their military power. In the world today, China has the largest military, followed by the United States of America. These two nations have an edge against some other nations in terms of their military power, though the largest is not the most powerful army today.

The armed forces of the nation form the defence of the nation from outside interference or inside security. The armed forces institution has the function of building an effective, capable, and efficient military that is needed to protect a given nation from invasion, whether from internal or external forces. Therefore, this institution, which is of great importance in a given state and nation, is to maintain the existence of the land.

During the colonial days, the imperialists have maintained grip and control over other people's lives and resources through the power of their military institutions. All around the world, Europeans were able to run and control people by the power of their military or armed forces.

The continent of Africa was a victim of this, and that is why we need to build and maintain an effective, strong, and efficient armed forces in our different nations. The need of this institution cannot be toiled with or neglected. Intervention that has been carried out in recent years in warring African nations has succeeded with some countries' military powers being injected in these warring states, which helped to subdue rebels, radicals, and disgruntled elements that were destabilising our continent with unnecessary wars.

The Economic Community Cease-Fire Monitoring Group (ECOMOG) military contingents, assembled by the Economic Community of West African States (ECOWAS), were successful in stopping wars in Liberia and Sierra Leon, to mention a few. Even under the auspices of the African Union (AU) or the Organisation of African Unity, countries such as Angola, Somalia, and others are test cases where the presence of some nations' military powers have been of paramount importance in saving lives and ending and stabilising warring factions in the African continent. Therefore, we need the armed forces of the people and not the armed forces against the people.

However, we in Africa know that our military or armed forces carry the stamp of the colonial past. So our present armed forces need to be transformed into the people's army—that is to say, the army that should protect them, not the one that tends to destroy them. The armed forces in our different nations should have unity, love, and cooperation between them and the people they serve.

The armed forces needed in our continent today is one that must rid themselves of brutality, starchiness, and rigid class distinctions, which are the hallmarks of the army enthroned in our system. They should learn how to ensure that their members never harass, intimidate, or maltreat fellow citizens, that they never loot the people's property, that they respect the women of society, that they pay a fair price for whatever services given to them by their fellow citizens. There is this attitude by the Nigerian police force and military of not paying for services rendered to them by civilians. When they join commercial vehicles, they never agree to pay even though they know quite well that it is not for free. In fact, I don't know if this is the case in some other African nations. If it is, there is a need for all of them to change this attitude and embrace the new way in which armed forces in the developed world live and conduct themselves.

The armed forces in the continent should understand that military intervention has derailed democracy and aspirations of the people of Africa to enjoy a full democracy. However, there might be cases when they have to intervene to bring order in society. But their intervention should be without the agenda to rule, but to bring peace and stability. The transition period should be short, where an election will be organised and monitored by them so that there would be no malpractice during this democratic process. Their duty is to defend and protect her citizens from external attacks and halt internal disturbances. The armed forces in many developed democracies have shown how the armed forces should function.

Health Institution / Healthcare

This means a public or nonprofit organisation within the state that provides healthcare and related services, including but not limited to the provision of inpatient and outpatient care, diagnostic or therapeutic services, laboratory services, medical drugs, nursing care, assisted living, and elderly care and housing (including retirement communities and equipment used). It can also been seen as the provision of healthcare and related services (Oregon legislature). Also, the health institution is dedicated to the provision of healthcare facilities such as hospitals and ambulatory surgical centres (*Wikipedia*).

Health institutions in any given country are required to make provisions for the prevention of diseases, illnesses, injuries, and other physical and mental impairments in human healthcare. This institution is organised and established to meet the health needs of the larger population. The institution of health has to be made more central amongst government as well as market participation, though market participation makes it expensive, corrupt, and fraudulent.

According to the World Health Organization (WHO), a well-functioning healthcare or health institution system requires a financing mechanism, workforce, reliable information on which to base decisions and policies, and well-maintained facilities and logistics to deliver quality medicines and technology. This institution, in fact, can form a significant part of a country's economy, just like in the United States with Medicare/Medicaid. Under the health institution insurance scheme, many jobs and wealth are created (e.g. in the Netherlands' economy is a compulsory insurance scheme under the health ministry/institution).

In 2008, for example, the healthcare or health institution industry consumed an average of 9 per cent of the gross domestic product (GDP) across most developed Organisation for Economic Co-operation and Development (OECD) countries: US, 16 per cent; France, 11 per cent; and Switzerland, 10.7 per cent. These were the top three spenders in the healthcare institution.

A well-funded and well-established healthcare institution is one of the most important areas of development in every nation in the world. The continent of Africa has lacked this for years, and that needs to change in this new age. The large wealth accruing from our different countries' resources should be channelled into building and maintaining a strong institution such as that of healthcare. The importance of this can no longer be left at the mercy of corrupt political rulers who have no vision to propel the continent to a better future in the world stage.

I still go back to the achievement made by John Kufuor, the former president of Ghana, in creating a health insurance scheme in Ghana and also to a recent approach by Uhuru Kenyatta of Kenya, though that of Kenyatta is not a perfect system because it is not sustainable since women will obtain healthcare for free. We need a robust and well-funded health scheme subsidised by the state, where citizens will still pay and receive quality, reasonable, and affordable healthcare that is durable, regardless of which political party comes into power.

The state or nation owes her citizens the right to maintain their health and physical well-being, which has to be their concern and responsibility. The different nations in the continent of Africa will and should at all times strive to provide medical services to or for all her citizens. There should be enough resources made available by each and every nation or state, which will enable her to wage continuous fights against epidemic and endemic diseases, both present and emerging. The health institution has the responsibility as a state apparatus to provide information to the citizens about hygienic living. It has to develop and promote social and preventive medicines as well as set up sanatoriums for incurable and infectious diseases and mental cases and good networking of maternity homes for the ante- and postnatal care of mothers. The need for a clean and healthy environment should be part of education programmes by the health institution to every citizen so that the consciousness of keeping the environment clean is established. This will help reduce environment pollution, which will be a source of disease and illness to the people.

A strong and formidable foundation on health should be laid to stand the test of time, not a haphazard approach that will last a while and collapse within decades. I still remember in the late 1970s and early 1980s as a primary school boy witnessing and visiting a dispensary unit in my community, but today, that health institutional unit has disappeared from every part of Nigeria. However, you see people parading themselves as commissioners and ministers for health without having a single idea what health ministry is all about. When some of them get sick, they want to be flown overseas to receive medical treatment, whereas others like them work for the good of their citizens to establish and maintain worthy and durable health institution for the benefit of all. In fact, I do get happy when some die seeking medical help abroad. Let us think and invest in building a quality health institution in our respective nations and the continent. This will help us to curb diseases and save the lives of our citizens as well as create a lot of employment.

As was said earlier, the health institution is an engine of economic growth and an employment avenue that helps the government reduce unemployment over a long time. In the area of healthcare financing, Ronald J. Vogel proposed that it is better to shift public financing resources from the hospital sector to primary and preventive care in order to reposition financial resources away from the colonial period and postcolonial concentration upon cost-ineffective hospitals. This goes back to what was said above about primary and preventive healthcare. Those in charge of heath institutions in the continent of Africa should do more in this area. They must try to find the best way to handle health issues in the continent as a whole in order to make progress in the health sector.

Personnel

Health workers such as nurses, doctors, pharmacists, and public health officials should be well informed on the issues of new technological development in handling and treating diseases emerging in the continent. On the other hand, their respective governments should empower these health workers by improving the condition of their services. They need to give them the tools they require to deliver quality healthcare to the citizens, which should not be limited by government policies and the careless attitude of neglect and lack of seriousness on the side of those in authority.

In recent years, the continent of Africa has been losing this group of health personnel to the West because of immigration. A lot trained health workers in the continent of Africa have migrated to the developed nations where pay, the condition of services, and tools and equipment needed for their services are provided to them.

This is still ongoing because many of our young health workers want to leave today and tomorrow to seek for the greener pastures of the West. The governments have to discourage them by improving their pay and providing good working conditions so that they can function effectively and efficiently in caring for their own people rather than taking their services outside the shores of their fatherland.

Let us do something now for today and a better future for the children of Africa so that we can enjoy quality healthcare and that our health providers will be happy to render the services they were trained to do.

The Institution of Labour and Productivity

This is one of the most important institutions in many nations for the government to fulfil his duty to the citizens of a given state. It is responsible for matters concerning employment and labour, legislation affecting employment and labour, as well as matters relating to labour relations and trade. The labour institution is also seen to be a partner organ comprising employer representatives, worker representatives, government representatives, and independent members appointed by the Ministry of Labour.

Most of the developed nations such as the UK, US, France, Germany, Australia, and Canada do not toil with this institution or ministry because it plays a great role in the economy of the nation, with labour peace being very essential for the prosperity of any given economy. When there is labour union unrest in any given state, the economy is in jeopardy. It is the duty of this institution to train, educate, and put people in study and research in labour-related subjects, which the states later benefits from by tapping into talents from these to employ in different disciplines. The institution mediates between industries and workers as well as employers and employees in creating good understanding between the two bodies, without which there will chaos in the working conditions between them.

The last time President Barack Obama was in Africa, he emphasised the importance of a strong, efficient, and effective institution as a way to further progress. Most of these institutions we are talking about are in existence in the continent of Africa, but the lack of efficiency and do not make it possible to fulfil the objectives of its creation. Therefore, we need reforms and technocrats who are sincere and patriotic to the fatherland/motherland to manage these institutions so that the citizenry of a given nation in particular and the continent in general can benefit from these institutions. This in turn will elevate our continent to compete with other continents around the globe.

Functions of the Ministry of Labour

The different ministries of labour around the world have more or less similar functions, though their activities vary from country to country. Some expanded their areas of jurisdiction. The following are the most important functions common to many nations:

1. Enforce compliance with employment laws (international labour standards and codes of practices as well as reviewing of labour standards and domestication of conventions and recommendations)
2. Provide social security
3. Plan development and promotion of effective utilisation of human resources
4. Ensure availability of skilled manpower for industries
5. Maintain stable industrial relations through early apprehension and resolutions of disputes

It provides publications and services to help employees and employers understand their rights and obligations. It organises information seminars and workshops for employer groups, employment counsellors, and professional associations. It also reviews employment standards, conducts inspections, etc.

The functions and activities of this institution are enormous, which cannot be completely shared in this book. As you read through this work, I believe you will be exposed to other functions of the Ministry of Labour around the globe. The major point here is to let our policymakers and citizens understand that there are rights and obligations for the government and citizens that need to be looked into and addressed so as to move Africa forward.

The state owes the citizens a lot through this intuition in order to create a viable environment that is good for industrial development, economic growth, and improvement in the standard of living. If the working conditions are good, labour laws and standards are maintained, and good wages are given, then workers and families will have good life.

Merely looking at this institution, we can say that a lot is required by the Ministry of Labour and Development or the institution of labour in gearing a lot of countries in the continent forward. As mentioned earlier in this chapter about other institutions, their viability also depends on this ministry in raising quality workers through training, education, and innovation. In a country like Nigeria, the most populated black nation on earth, the Ministry of Labour and Productivity has failed to live to its expectations since it has remained nonviable in the eyes of many in the nation because of its lessened activity in performing its goals or functions.

There is an urgent need in the continent of Africa to let different institutions of labour and productivity know exactly how important this ministry is in the development and growth of the economy of each nation they serve or represent. They have to understand that it is their responsibility to generate employment and create an enabling environment for national growth.

The Ministry of Labour has to have a purpose to grow the economy of the nation for all citizens. It has to have the responsibility of helping businesses become more productive and internationally competitive and, by so doing, create opportunities for all citizens to contribute to the economy. The Ministry of Labour should also be providing more jobs and increasing productive opportunities for citizens. It has to ensure that citizens participate in more productive and higher-paid work. Growth for all means providing better-quality housing that is safe and affordable for all citizens and not for the selected few, as is the case in many African countries.

We know that the ministry cannot provide jobs for everyone, but its actions and policies can create an environment where some can create jobs for themselves in the private sector. The action of the ministry in adapting to new methodologies in innovation can spur economic growth and development, which is desperately needed in the continent. Let us think and work hard in this area to help bring about growth and development.

A man willing to work but cannot find one is the greatest type of inequality under the sun. So let us make good use of this ministry as it is the developed nations to create jobs and empower our people to make a better life and usher in a new hope for the continent with all our God-given resources. It is also imperative that this ministry invest more in human resources development so that we will not continue to depend on the outside world, such as China, to come and harness our resources for us because of the lack of human resources.

These institutions and others like them should be the focus of different governments in the continent of Africa individually as well as collectively to bring about a new direction, thinking, and methodology to usher in development. The essentiality of a strong and efficient institution in the continent shouldn't be a thing to continue to be toiled with by political leaders of our time. Many historians or economists in the continent can vividly remember how Kwame Nkrumah of Ghana appointed Sir William Arthur Lewis of Saint Lucia in 1957 as an economic adviser to the newly independent state of Ghana. Sir Lewis had to develop a five-year plan (1959–1964) for the economic development of the developing nation. Such men with vision are what is needed today in Africa to move the continent forward for a better tomorrow.

Our civil servants who happen to control or manage our existing institutions should have a sense of nationalism and patriotism in running these institutions so that they can be better managed for the benefit of the citizenry of the nations where they are in charge.

The mentality of communalism should be their watchword or motto rather than that of selfish ambitions, where they want to rule and die and the positions remains available only to their children and grandchildren, as has been enshrined in the African system. The idea to raise new technocrat and quality administrators should be a thing of great urgency in the continent if we really want to move forward like other continents.

The objectives of organisations such as New Partnership for Africa's Development (NEPAD) and African Development Bank (ADB) should be a thing of implementation and not only exist on the pages of newspapers and on television screens. Policy initiatives that are working better in some countries in the continent should be copied and applied in other nations to improve the quality of lives and empower citizens. Too much bureaucracy that serves as a bottleneck or hampers effective functioning of institutions has to be done away with. Political parties that come to power should not be interested in introducing their own projects in the interest of party politics but rather should continue existing ones that are beneficial to the growth of the nations and the benefit of the citizens. The ideal political party agenda has negative effects on the functioning of our institutions. Good quality, efficient, and effective managers of institutions are moved around or removed for the interest of party politics instead of the interest of the nation. Some of these things are killing and hampering our institutions that are greatly needed for a better Africa.

CHAPTER 4

Independence and Its Effects on the Continent

After the slave trade, the Europeans discovered minerals in many parts of the African continent, and their greedy desire and exploitation increased. The Europeans became impatient because the Africans wanted to take control of their kingdom and resources by themselves. This made the Europeans complain about taxes the African kings levied on the minerals they were taking and other restrictions by the kings. Because of this, by the middle of the eighteenth century, the Europeans conspired to take control or annex Africa so that they could have total and absolute control over the people and their resources. This brought them to their colonisation agenda, and the people lost their independence.

Great Britain, France, Germany, Portugal, Belgium, Italy, and the Netherlands took hold of the continent, its people, and their resources. Now the mineral resources they used to take and pay taxes for became their own possession. They subjected the people to their own control, and their resources finally became theirs to manage. They reaped the rewards of what they didn't sow. This brought agony and destruction to the continent of Africa. In fact, the dispossession of Africans from their wealth and resources lasted for more than two hundred years. The Africans struggled to resist the annexing of their land and resources by the European invaders, but the cost was much, though the resistance brought an end to the colonisation by the Europeans after a very long time.

The decolonisation of the African continent followed the world war as the colonised people agitated for independence and withdrawal of colonial powers and their administration over their territories. The then Soviet Union and China supported Africans for their demand for independence, though these two were also working for their own interests as they were in war with the West. Though these two blocks supported Africans for their demand for independence, without the hard effects of the world war on the West, it would have been very difficult for the continent of Africa in the struggle for liberation. The war put the West in economic hardship that they were mainly unable to continue to finance and run the colonies. Finally, they decided to give the Africans autonomy but still wanted to run them from both outside and within (neocolonialism, as Frantz Fanon and his friends called it). This has been the case even till today since the West most of the time decides who rules a particular country in the continent, how much of our resources we sell to them, etc. We are in a way independent in our political, economic, and cultural lives; but the effects and influence of the colonial powers are still prominent in a lot of our daily activities.

The decolonisation process is still not complete until Africa becomes completely liberated mentally, politically, culturally, and economically, like China and other nations who can now run things on their own, completely free from Western interference and dictates. By the time Africa reaches this point, we can actually be independent and free from a lot of control from the West and the rest of the world. The moment we are able to achieve this, then Africa will be on its way forward and can compete on the international stage with other continents of the world.

True independence means freedom from control, support, aid, and subjection. After the struggles against colonisation, the West gave us half independence and maintained halfway control on us. Even when they tend to leave us alone, our greedy political leaders sell themselves to the West by aligning with them to maintain their grip on power. They turn into dictators, using the system of brute and oppressive force of the former oppressors to humiliate, dictate, and control their own brothers and sisters. The transferred effects of the old colonial syndromes remain in place, and this has limited most, if not all, states in the continent from moving forward in realising the whole dream of being free from colonialism.

The corrupt and brutal attitude of the powers left behind has continued to haunt Africa in oblivion since she is dominated with wars, nepotism, corruption, anarchy, hunger, and chaos from one region to the other. Powers were left in the hands of the few raised by the colonial powers, with the idea of the few dominating the majority. It has become a disease that has refused to respond to vaccine that would destroy the epidemic situation that needs to be halted before it spreads.

The decolonisation struggle paved the way for independence per se; and many African countries were partly set free from total control over their territories, resources, and people. It was a great achievement in that most of them got the independence without a gun being fired. However, many others suffered, paying with their blood before having a taste of freedom from the colonial powers. All these combined should encourage Africans to work diligently to prove to themselves that they can manage their affairs effectively.

Saying that Africans were unable to manage their own affairs was part of the argument made by the colonial powers not to leave the people alone. People like Ian Smith of then Rhodesia made these claims to other people of like minds in the West. In fact, if Ian Smith were reincarnated today and saw the state of things and governance in Africa, he would proudly say, 'Look. Indeed, I was not completely wrong.' The struggle for and the gaining of independence were excellent occurrences in the continent of Africa. For more than five decades, we have been a people free from absolute control of other people over our daily lives, resources, decisions, etc. But the dividends of this freedom have eluded the general population of Africans. The people still live under dictators and corrupt political leaders who continue to mismanage the scanty or meagre resources left over by the colonial and neocolonial powers. The most painful thing in life is when your worst enemy happens to come from your own family. Those left to control and rule us have bankrupted the nations with their greed and lack of vision for tomorrow. They want to live and die for themselves, like most Negroes do. This attitude has hindered forward and innovative actions that are needed in the continent.

Was Independence a Positive or a Negative Change?

This is a million-dollar question that might be answered correctly since many can put up an argument to support their view. Many may see the current state of affairs in the continent and always say that it is a positive thing, while others disagree. The fact that African people could break the shackles of absolute control other people had over their daily lives is and should be a positive thing. Many who lived under or are still living under occupied power were never content or happy. Even animals always resist other foreign or external animals invading their areas of domain. The insistence shows that in this case, your movement and source of livelihood are to be reordered or inhibited.

Presently, the situations in Iraq, Palestine, Afghanistan, and Chechnya are evident of living and being controlled by others. Regardless of how nice an occupier may be, the resentment will always be there. It is a natural phenomenon that both man and animal want freedom. Consider your dog. If you chain her for some time, anytime you release her, she will show an expression of relief and joy. This is one of the episodes of Africa before and after independence. The continent was free and living their lives freely, orderly, and harmoniously till, suddenly, the West meddled in and changed the dynamics of the people.

The advent of the West or Europeans in the continent disoriented many people, making them become disjointed and lack cohesion and ushering an aggressive attitude in them. These have dominated the lives of Africans since and after independence. The white man's idea of the use of brutal force introduced in Africa has had great negative effects on the continent even as of today. The gaining of independence made the people of Africa rejuvenate their God-given pride as humans and people endowed with God-given potentials to excel in their endeavours. Independence made us feel as part of the community since many countries around the world at the time have been free from foreign domination, partly in the sense of being able to decide for themselves how to run their own affairs. Being under occupation or taken as slaves wasn't something only particular to Africans. The Jews were the earliest slaves in history, both as indicated in the Bible and their history in the Spanish, Italian, and French enclave of 1242. African slavery started in the eighteenth century and a little earlier before that, initiated by the Arab Muslim expansion. So Africans should dominate their lives but continue to feel victims as slaves, which has also hampered their development as individuals and as a people.

The greatest country in the world today, the United States of America, was also colonised by the same Europeans who took hold of Africa. The United States fought for the same independence we fought for, but after gaining independence, it has grown beyond the negative effects of being controlled and run by others as the Africans were. Independence is an opportunity for you to make your life better and more productive, but Africans have failed in capitalising on this opportunity. Those that were given the mantle of leadership to lead us have failed in their responsibility to bring Africa to a position in the world stage when they used to be on equal footing with the Europeans before the West began to see us as second-class people as of late eighteenth century.

In 1684, a Gold Coast (Ghana) delegation received the cold shoulder from Europeans for the first time. The delegation representatives were eighty-six rulers of the country who for nearly four hundred years had been recognised in Europe as kings. These kings came to the residence of the great elector Frederick William of Brandenburg, only to be treated with little regard. These kings were registered as 'chiefs', a relegation that suggested or denoted lower class or primitivism. (See *Darkest Europe and Africa's Nightmare* by Akinyi von K'Orinda-Yimbo.)

Each of the leaders of the Ghana delegation were registered as 'Jan Janke' in the official documents of Germany. This step was taken since they felt that their African names were not worth mentioning. This visit in 1684 gave birth to the first Brandenburg colony in Africa. From this time onwards, the Europeans began to treat Africans as second class and no longer as the partners they used to be. In fact, Africans have acted in good faith and were trustful, but the Europeans have been treacherous and have always had the idea of conquest and dispossession.

The betrayal of Africans by the West is rarely spoken of by the West apologists. Anyway, it should have served Africans better not to trust the West and instead work hard for her own interest and that of her people.

Independence and Democracy

Freedom from outside control ushered in the word 'democracy': the government of the people, by the people, and for the people. But has this been the case in Africa since after the struggle for and gaining of independence? The freedom to rule and control our own lives has not been realised in the true sense. The West left power in the hands of their puppets who more or less work to maintain their influence on the continent. The proxy control using African political leaders as stooges has been more harmful and detrimental to the continent than when they were fully in charge of the continent. Many might agree with me, but some also might not. When the West was in charge, you could openly see their crimes and accuse them of illegality and foul play; but when they remote things to their advantage from faraway capitals, you can't clearly point accusing fingers anymore.

Neocolonialism has been the real problem to the continent of Africa, crippling her to her knees through marginalisation, instigating instability, as well as controlling our resources in terms of market and economic policies.

The late Fela Anikulapo Kuti of Nigeria calls it 'democrazy' instead of 'democracy'. The leaders of democracy in Africa have made the word 'democracy' nonsense since most people in the African continent have never enjoyed it in full or have been touched by the real effects of it.

We have been run and ruled by the few cabals and clienteles who have no regard for the word 'democracy' and its real meaning. They steal the elections and even after stealing the rights of the people during voting, they become dictators by remaining in power forever. They treat the people with no respect and have no regard to international laws. When your vote doesn't count for whom you cast it, that is not democracy because you have been denied the right of your choice. The people's leaders such as Mugabe, Museveni, Omar Hassan al-Bashir, Paul Biya, and their fellow compatriots either dead or living are good examples of African independence and democracy. Many in Africa were born to meet these groups being in power and have today been able to contest with the same group in the field of elections. Their brutal use and application of force to quench upcoming brain for change or opposition can no more be even compared with the brutality of the colonial masters against those who opposed their continuous control of different lands in Africa during the colonial era. For instance, the Mau Mau of Kenya, early African National Congress (ANC) activists, were tortured to death or castrated for their demand of independence and democracy. Many of them who paid highly under the colonial Europeans are suffering more today under the leadership of their fellow compatriots or even those who made no contribution or paid a price for freedom.

If well analysed, these issues were attitudes copied or learned from the history of the colonial authorities who used brutal force. They employed a divide-and-rule tactic and racism to raise and feed this group of African political leaders and their political successors. They have always patronised those leaders who served their interests rather than the interests of the people. They have worked to maintain them in power regardless of what the citizens say or feel about these leaders. The Mobutus, Kabilas, Mubaraks, Kagamis—these classes of people remain the darlings of the West so long as their interests are served or protected, and the rest of us become figures that don't count. The meaning of 'democracy' can be redefined to suit the Western opinion. The government of the people, by the people, and for the people in all its genuine meaning has eluded the continent of Africa.

One-Party System

The trend of democratisation has created room for dominant parties and a dominant party system in Africa. Analyses show that about fifty-nine elections result in eighteen sub-Saharan African countries shows that there is a problem in an effective number of the classification of parties; and where it might exist, it is flawed. The party that tries to come to power has tried to reduce other rivalries through a one-party system. This means that in the parliament, there will be little or no opposition. Every politician who wants to be in parliament must be a member of the ruling party.

Most of the time, the idea of a one-party system or one-party dominance has lead to dictatorship in the long run. The ZANU PF of Zimbabwe under Mugabe has dominated the political party politics of the nation since its independence. The same is also the case in Eritrea, where the president has remained in power ever since its independence. The Peoples Democratic Party (PDP) in Nigeria has turned the country into a virtually one-party state. Over the last sixteen years, the party has become dominant not because of its excellent performance, but through flawed electoral processes. The idea of dominance copied from the colonial authorities became entrenched in our so-called democracy through a one-party system. In fact, this has been the problem of the nations in the continent of Africa.

Multiparty elections do not lead automatically to a multiparty system. In sub-Saharan African nations, the spread of multiparty politics in the 1990s has given rise to dominant parties. Most African states have employed multiparty elections, but no change in government (Bratton and Van de Walle 1997; Baker 1998; Herbst 2001; Cowen and Laakso 2002). In a situation where changes have taken place in government, the opposition is by no means entrenched in power. The has actually created a model of one-party 'dominance' (O'Brien 1999). By the end of 1990, many observers expressed concern about the idea of one-party regimes in Africa. This looks like the situation after independence, where many of the leaders perpetuated themselves in power.

According to Peter Anyang' Nyong'o from Kenya, African single- or one-party regimes argue that traditional African societies were used to one-party systems. Those who support this view forgot that political parties as such did not exists in so-called traditional African societies. Therefore, logically speaking, the concept of a political party cannot be used in the analysis of politics in such societies. Those who approve or benefit from a one-party system on the basis of our cultural heritage have therefore been doing so by means of false analogies and use of anachronism.

The advent of European colonialism brought several changes in the structure and dynamics of African societies. Amongst these was the introduction of production for market, superintended by the modern state, complete with all its complex institutions of power and authority as well as its demand that society produce surpluses sufficient enough to maintain administrative and ideological superstructure.

However, there was a general resistance of the African societies against the establishment of a state structure that engaged in political oppression and the economic exploitation of the people. The colonial powers were forced to modify its attitude, though she recruited several indigenous elements to carry out its administration. Some of these elements were later to become the leaders of the African societies. This has affected independence and democracy in various, if not all, African states. The idea of a single- or one-party type of democracy has killed development, progress, and innovation. The economic theory of the 'the law of diminishing returns' becomes active in these long-term one-party leaders in Africa. The longer they stay in power, the less productive, innovative, and progressive they become.

In this situation, they become more afraid to leave office for fear of prosecution. When this sets in, the now dictators turn to the use of brutal force to subdue or oppress any opposition in sight. They apply all tactics and methods of oppression in resisting change that might usher a new idea and brain for power change and an enabling system that will benefit the citizens. In fact, the worst is that the apologists of this group of men see no wrong in what their masters, tribes, and clienteles do that are detrimental to the development of the nation state. Most of the time, it is only when their boss falls—maybe by death or by means of removal, if possible by a revolution type as in Tunisia, Egypt, Libya, etc.—that the then beneficiaries will begin to talk nonsense against their one-time allies. These factors and other negatives that accompany African independence and democracy have delayed and continue to delay the forward movement that is greatly needed in the African continent.

There is a need to kill and destroy the one-party system of democratic nature of politics entrenched in African states since independence. The growth of a multiparty system should be encouraged and fought for so that the citizenry of Africa could see a new type of democratic structure where the real feeling of independence might emerge. Civil societies have to stand up for both their civil and political rights as citizens of any given state and demand for change in a new direction. When these changes can be achieved, it's going to empower us to make progress in many institutional areas of the society.

From Democracy to Dictatorship

When the British and the French colonialists pulled out of Africa, it is like they left modern democracy in place in the continent. But within a couple of years, majority of the so-called democracy or democratic states disappeared. It rather created a place with an authoritarian type of government or a 'one-party' system that is a regular right of dictators. A number of changes took place, such as military coup d'état, in order to unseat the dictators. Many were amazed at how fast the democratic lands or countries turned to dictatorship after independence. The answer was clear—since the colonial government was in the form of dictatorship for more than a hundred years, it did little to develop a democratic structure that would suit the traditional setting that was there before their advent. Just close before independence, they voted for the stationing of African political parties, and these parties had no real solid political basis to champion democracy in the continent. In fact, this brought in the single- or one-party system oriented towards dictatorship. Some argue in favour of dictatorship as being durable and able to foster long-term development. But this has not been the case in Africa.

In the case of Malaysia, Mahathir Mohamad became a success after twenty years of being in power. He transformed Malaysia into a modern democratic state and improved its economy as well as infrastructure. Unfortunately, none of the African dictators have been able to transform any given state where they have dominated power for two to three decades. There is a need to bring change and to stop the continuance of one-party dominance that is ruining the life and society of African nations.

If you travel around the continent of Africa, from north to south and east to west, the situation has remained the same. Tragic.

During the colonial days and their embedded system of dictatorship, educated Africans, both at home and abroad, united to forge a common front to liberate her people from the shackles of oppression, intimidation, and domination from foreign occupation. They fought to have access to and control of their resources. This paid off after the struggle and resistance against the invaders when they finally got independence to manage their own affairs. Unfortunately, there was a new type of dominance, intimidation, corruption, and control over the citizens of Africa. This new control, now perpetrated by their own, needs also to be resisted again if possible, jointly, like pre-independence Africa; or the resistance should be carried out in country to country with joint and integrated effort to rid the country or continent of its new dictators and dominant individuals as well as political parties that have limited the progress of the people.

The idea of Arab Spring started in the northern part of the continent of Africa (Tunisia) and since then has expanded to most of the Arab regions. Since the African dictators don't want to leave power in peace or modernise our society, then they should be forced to leave in pieces. We should rejuvenate the same spirit that was used to resist and drive the colonial masters away from the control of our resources and daily lives. The Dutch say 'Als Ze wil niet Luisteren, Ze moet Horen'—that is to say, 'If they don't want to listen, then they will see action'.

However, some might say that you are preaching violence; but if this group of politicians do not want to leave power and make way for new ones, then we have to drive them out of that seat. Gaddafi never believed that he would leave power, but today, he is resting in peace. So shall be the fate of the others like him who do not want to leave power. The wind of change is blowing, and the sub-Saharan Africans should emulate other revolutionaries and fight for change in their region. It is better to die for a reason while fighting than to die for nothing through these criminals' bad governance and dictatorship that have hindered our forward movement like those of other continents of the world.

Independence is a good thing in the sense that it offers a good opportunity for freedom to develop and enhance ourselves for a better tomorrow. In the case of sub-Saharan African, it brought misery, disease, and lack of development, progress, and innovation.

It is sad that even over three decades since the colonial masters left Africa, no African nation in the continent has added a new railway line to the ones left by the colonialists, not even having discussed creating or building one to connect one end of the province to the other. For instance, Nigeria, with all the oil wealth she has, has been unable to develop a common efficient and effective railway system to move its people and goods around the nation.

The countries of sub-Saharan Africa have made independence seem like a thing of regret to many. It is freedom of being able to control and manage your own affairs to your own benefit, thereby improving your well-being. But in our case, it looks like it would have been better to remain under colonial rule. That would have offered people a lot of chances, better education, healthcare services, and a host of other social services states provide for its citizens. During colonial times, these services were guaranteed for those who were willing to take the opportunity. Our own political leaders have turned to be the enemies of the state and the people by holding us hostage. We lack quality education, health services, transportation systems, etc. We have been limited from development by our own (to be modified later).

CHAPTER 5

Conflict and Resolution

The continent of Africa has become synonymous with violence, hunger, and intractable conflicts as known to the West and other parts of the world. Everyone around the world, both the intellectuals and not alike, can refer to Africa and Africans as such even though Africans are better in all ramifications and sense of quality life and education. Since the advent of the Europeans, with their long years of slave trade, partitioning, and imperial control over Africa, the continent has never known peace. This conflict, initiated partly by the West through the outcome of the Berlin Conference of 1885 and subsequent partitioning, has generated unending conflict in the continent.

In the beginning of the early 1960s, many states in the continent began to gain independence from the West so that they could manage their own affairs. But after the early years of independence, African nations has fallen into long conflicts with no end in sight. The menace of wars, violence, and conflicts has derailed the needed development and improvement in the lives of the people, as was anticipated during the struggle for independence. It is like Africa stepped into the shoes of Eastern Europe (Balkan) and Latin America, with their history an unending battles and collisions between states, tribes, etc. The continent became a lucrative market for the West to dump or test their newly manufactured weaponry since most of them have reconciled their own antagonisms amongst themselves. Their instigation and our own foolishness not to learn from our own history have made it impossible for the continent to free herself from this ugly thing called conflict/war.

A good observer in the partitioning of Africa by the West during the colonial era might be well aware that conflict, violence, and war are inevitable in the sense that through the partitioning, families or tribes were once made to stay apart from their brothers and forced to join others of different cultural heritage, so to say. A typical example is the old Senegal-Gambia later splinted into Senegal and Gambia, where people of the same family happened to find themselves living in different countries. This was not by choice, but rather by force; in that case, how is it possible that there will be no acrimony amongst the people?

However, whatever the wrongs of the West were, we Africans need to come to terms that we all have to find a way to reunite and live in peace with one another. A lot of examples of this type of division and merging people of different orientations and cultures continue to play a part in the unending conflict in Africa, coupled with other factors instituted by the West when they hastily left African leadership in the hands of the sycophants and sympathisers. It has also made it sometimes near impossible in finding solutions and resolving some of Africa's regional, intrastate, and communal conflicts. In recent years, we have acknowledged great achievements in the direction of conflict management and resolution in the continent regardless of the odds facing her in complete conflict resolution and postconflict reconstruction, which will help minimise the emergence of the same conflict. Conflict management and resolution ideas are greatly needed in the continent so that we will be able to overcome this menace that has limited the forward movement the continent requires to grow in all areas of life's endeavours.

In fact, somehow somebody might ask, 'What is conflict, and how does it begin in the first place?' It is a pertinent question to ask, and it is of great importance that it is defined for readers to know and be able to avoid it or limit getting in conflict with others—be it in the state, parties, tribes, communities, and even amongst friends and families. 'Conflict' is coming into collision or disagreement, being contradictory, at variance or in opposition, a clashing state, often prolonged fighting, a battle or a war. It can also mean a being in a state of disharmony between incompatible ideas or interests. However, these might not offer the best definition of what 'conflict' is, but they help us have a clue of what it is.

In looking at Hobbes's realism, according to Lorenz (1997), violence or conflict in human beings is caused by man's natural inclination to aggressiveness or situations that provoke aggressiveness. On the other hand, Burton has a similar opinion to Lorenz when it comes to conflict, saying that the human impulse to sin, aggression, or dominance cannot be stamped out; it requires control or balancing by a countervailing force (2009). Here, he points out that aggression and domination by some over others can cause conflict; he went further to say that we can overcome conflict by avoiding aggressiveness, applying control, and using of counterforce to eliminate or reduce violence and conflict.

The idea of inequality in many areas of life contributes more in the origin of violence as well as conflict and war. The need for equal treatment to all and the maintenance of justice around the world will help mankind limit conflict. Africa is bearing the brunt of unending conflict in the recent years as a result of all these factors indicated above. We, therefore, need measures to help us limit conflict and its root causes so that we may enjoy enduring peace in the continent.

According to information shared by B. V. Ihejiaku and J. Dawdu, since independence, Africa has been engulfed in intractable conflicts that threaten the peace and the stability of the continent. These conflicts and violence have increased since the late 1980s through early 1990 and to date. The unending raging conflicts in the continent, coupled with bad governance, have impeded progress.

Statistics show that there have been 116 recorded conflicts since the end of the world war. These conflicts have increased in scale in the continent of Africa more than any other place in world, mostly since the 1980s and 1990s (Uppsala Conflict Data Program (UCDP)). Of all the 116 wars that existed between the Cold War and 2003, only seven of it have been between states, 109 of it have been internal, and Africa had thirty-two of these wars between 1989 and 2003. Information obtained from a UN Office on Drugs and Crime (UNODC) study concerning conflict around the world conducted by the University of Maryland's Center for International Development and Conflict Management found that thirty-three nations are at great risk for instability. And of these thirty-three nations mentioned, twenty are in the continent of Africa (Dane 2001; Kaplan 1994). In a widely read, but controversial essay written by Kaplan in 1994, 'The Coming of Anarchy', he predicted the fragility in many African states because of political and social chaos and instability. Although the continent continues to clamour for the dire need of peace, it continues to witness a great number of conflicts. There are examples of continued conflicts in the continent, such as what happened in Kenya in 2007, in Mali, and in Zimbabwe in 2008.

The African continent has witnessed four types of conflicts and internal coup d'états, regional conflicts, and internal crises (violent demonstrations, riots, rampages, and communal clashes; see Ihejiaku 2009). Conflicts have destabilised many African nations and continue to destabilise them today.

According to Wayande, conflict has had enormous costs on the nations affected by it directly and other neighbours. These costs come in terms of loss of human life and property as well as destruction of social infrastructure (see Wayande 1997, page 20). Some of the countries affected by conflicts and disturbances include Nigeria (1967–1970, 1985–1993, and even presently in northern Nigeria), South Africa (1948–1994, riots and violent demonstrations), Angola (1975–2002), Rwanda (1990–2000), Liberia (1989–2000, both regional and internal conflicts), Sierra Leone (1991–2000), Democratic Republic of the Congo (1996–present), Sudan (1983–2009), and Somalia (1981–2002, some of these conflicts are even still ongoing with no end in sight). Some of the nations that seem like they are stable still have minor conflicts and oppression against the minority. For instance, Uganda and Kenya are facing upheavals. Kenya has had a lot of violent demonstrations in 1991, 1992, 1997, and between 2003 and 2008.

The continued conflicts and violence in Africa have reached an alarming rate; although some have been partially resolved, there is still a potential for emergence of new ones. There is a great increase in inequality, poverty, religious dissension, and safe havens for Arab and Islamic terrorists, as is seen in Mali, northern Nigeria, Libya, and Maghreb. The lack of complete control of borders and territories has increased the chances of transborder violence as well as terrorist activities. Governments should do more in improving governance and exercising their rights in protecting their citizens from the menace of terror and violence. The need for more regional military organs to protect the citizenry is of great importance in Africa. The formation of ECOMOG, a West African regional military force, has helped to quell wars and conflict in the subregions, such as Sierra Leone and Liberia. Another great example is the AU-organised force that works in collaboration with the UN and some European army that is helping in Somalia, Mali, Congo, Central African Republic, etc. More of this military unity is needed for a rapid reaction force to end conflicts in the African continent for the betterment and progress of our people. Peace brings in progress and development. The money Africa nations spend in buying weapons from the West to kill themselves can be invested in regional development, which will enable Africa to grow and become a continent with good stories and not only those of war and misery, as it has turned to be.

The UN and other international organisations should reach a strong binding consensus that will declare weapon sales to Africa as illegal, as they have declared on drugs. Weapons are more dangerous than drugs; but still, weapons are being sold to Africans to eliminate themselves each and every day in tribal, regional, and internal conflicts. The way the whole West united to end pirate activities in Somalia should be the same approach used to end weapon sales and conflicts in Africa. This is a must case in order to usher in a dispensation of peace with limited weapons of death and a reduction of conflicts in the continent.

A foul cry for deaths and destruction in Africa in terms of conflicts and violence can never be a solution; rather, reasonable action has to be taken so that Africa can enjoy peace, stability, and progress. Those merchants of flesh who engage in stirring up conflicts and violence for the sake of carting away raw materials and selling their outdated weapons for us to destroy ourselves should stop or be put on check by international law. Set Africa free from continued invasion and instigation of war and conflicts so that she can move forward and be able to enjoy her God-given potential, both in human and natural resources.

As I speak to the merchants of flesh, so do I speak to the dumb-headed African political rulers, not leaders—because if they were leaders, they would have led us to a great level of development since and after independence. Let Africans become conscious of who they are and also show a little patriotic attitude to the concerns of her citizenry in order to bring to a halt this conflict and violence that has dominated our continent since the advent of the white man's occupation. As we adopt this approach, I believe we can find a way forward to live in peace and harmony with one another. Conflict is like a snake's venom that destroys our society and hinders our progress.

Policy of Conflict Management and Intervention in Africa

The idea of conflict management and intervention should be paramount in both continental and international institutions-cum-organisations to lift off this menace of war and conflicts that has derailed this great continent for over ten decades. Regional as well as international organisations should make it an objective to intervene and manage conflicts and violence in Africa at the early stage rather than sit and watch until the Africans finish themselves off before intervening.

The stem has to be nipped in the bud before it grows. In fact, it has been unfortunate that the continent of Africa has become a battleground where the scramble to liquidate it continues, even after independence. Many around the world have escaped and emerged as people to be reckoned with in different factions. Vietnam and Cambodia as well as South American and Asian nations have overcome their odds. So why not Africa?

Positive intervention and conflict management, both from outside and continental bodies or organisations using forces in Africa, could manage rather than aggravate conflicts in Africa. Therefore, any of these two options is highly needed regardless of some associated disadvantages. Intervention is the best approach in order to prevent escalation whenever there is conflict or a violent eruption in a given state. So we need to get involved more in intervention at the early stage of conflict than wait till the last minute when souls have been lost. Rwanda was a good example of what is being spoken of here in terms of intervention and conflict management. Assuming the world intervened at the early stage of the conflict, that genocide wouldn't have taken place. Even today, many in the West still blame themselves for their failure, but that is medicine after death. It has always been the story of regret for not acting on time when it comes to Africa. A repetition was also seen in North and South Sudan and Darfur.

Skilled people who have a good knowledge and history of the people involved in conflict is of paramount importance to help in negotiation and communication between the parties involved in conflict. In this case, conflict managers need the following:

1. *Communication.* The warring parties involved in conflict need to be communicated the options involved in the conflict, which can help create a common promising frame or point of reference. Ann Daune, a behaviour expert, expresses that from the reference frame, you then work on resolving some of the matters. Further, you have to avoid making any promises in the beginning of conflict intervention; rather, make all parties involved understand the potential consequences of pursuing the conflict further. In some cases, understanding the consequences of the conflict might and can help expedite the resolution of the conflict. Perspective is of importance to access and be able to mediate a resolution. A conflict manager should be in a position to understand the perspective of each party involved. This idea is shared by management expert David A. Victor. For example, if the conflict is in the context of individuals, such as in a company between a manager and a subordinate, then the subordinate may be acting on fear rather than on rational thought. The manager might be using intimidation to get the results he wanted than being objective. In the case of nations, a stronger nation might apply the same tactics in order to achieve a better consensus than a weaker nation.

   Those working to resolve and manage conflicts must base their judgement on information that is comprehensive or interviews with the parties involved. Also, those doing the work of resolving and intervening must be resolute in presenting their solutions to the parties involved.

When applied before conflict escalates, this kind of approach makes more sense, and conflict that may linger for a longer period will be averted. Therefore, more intervention is needed. The use of forces is greatly needed so that talks will be followed by action to make conflict parties submit or meet their obligations as proposed by the conflict managers. The presence of forces can act as a barrier to limit the situation that would or might break out during negotiations between parties since interest in war might take advantage to create a fracas or violence.

Regional bodies as well as international organs or powerful states such as the United States, Britain, and the EU should not hesitate to release forces as well as finances to assist poor regional forces willing to do so in order to save lives and properties. The ECOMOG forces of West African states have demonstrated that this can be achieved when resources and the right approach are followed to stop conflict escalation. Africa needs more good integrated and concise efforts by the international community as well as regional bodies to make this a realistic goal. If this is done, then conflict in the continent may be a thing of the past or at least be reduced drastically. This will enhance nation-to-nation relationship and encourage regional development, which we so badly need to move forward. (Reconsider this part later, a mixed up of ideas)

2. *Intervention.* This is a combination of programme elements or strategies designed to produce behaviour changes or improve the health status amongst individuals or an entire population. Intervention may include educational programmes, new or stronger policies, improvements, or healthy promotion campaigns. Intervention that includes multiple strategies is typically an effective way in producing desired changes and lasting solutions or changes.

In the case of conflict intervention, we are looking to produce lasting solutions and changes that will help keep the peace for a long time. Intervention can be humanitarian or military/ force. Looking at the conflicts in Africa, intervention has not been taken seriously by those in authority, be it in the continent or the international community. It is of paramount importance that intervention becomes a necessary tool to end conflict and to stop the emergence of new ones. Intervention does try to find a way to stop a tense situation from escalating or growing into war or violence.

According to John M. Kabia, humanitarian intervention has long ago passed the airdropping of food to disaster-hit places or war torn-areas. We remember the days of humanitarian food intervention in Ethiopia, where food packages were airdropped. It occurred vividly again in southern Sudan, when war was ravaging the land. However, no matter what type it is, it is greatly needed in conflict-torn Africa to remedy and limit the suffering of the people. Both regional and international organisations need to have a strong agenda of earlier intervention in handling African areas of conflict.

Today, humanitarian intervention is about how to stop the slaughtering of civilians by machetes and guns as well as how to promote safety (provide safe havens) for war-ravaged women and children in areas of conflict in Africa and other places. Those involved in intervention have to be conscious and should be able to discern when to use force and when not to. John Kabia has shown concern in this area in conflict resolution. The international community must find an effective and efficient manner or way to solve complex political emergencies in Africa.

An abstract from John M. Kabia's study on conflict resolution in Africa enumerated some approaches, as has taken place in Sierra Leone, Liberia, Côte d'Ivoire (Ivory Coast), and Guinea-Bissau in West Africa. The ECOWAS has moved from being an economic integration to a strong regional security apparatus that has been able to intervene effectively in limiting conflicts in the subregion. The use of ECOMOG forces as part of the ECOWAS military/security unit to tackle regional conflict has proved that Africans, when serious and have the well-built capacity, can solve most of its problems without foreign intervention. Their performance in quelling the conflict in Liberia, Sierra Leone, as well as the Ivory Coast is an example of what can be achieved if we work together with genuine mind and intentions towards our brothers who need us in times of difficulty. Joseph Bangura expressed his impression of the positive feeling about the achievement of ECOMOG and ECOWAS in handling some of the regional issues. In this context, the whole African continent should copy and apply the ECOWAS strategy in all conflicts in Africa to bring to a stop the number of existing conflicts and emerging ones.

African organisations should be willing to intervene in time to limit violence, deaths, displacement, and destruction ruining the lives of citizens from time to time. Regional bodies have to meet from time to time to look at issues of concern that might ignite new conflicts in the regions.

We know that organisations such as ECOWAS and its security unit ECOMOG may have their own problems that have limited them from completely performing to the satisfaction of many.

This can be corrected if the international community—the US, EU, and UN—will continue to support them to build their capacity in many areas. The international community has to give them strong support in terms of financial resources, equipment, arms, etc. These can motivate and give them strong influence and position when it comes to intervention in separating warring parties. A well-built capacity will empower them to be more effective and efficient even when stronger parties are involved in the conflict.

Another great example of what regional bodies can achieve in Africa in terms of intervention occurred in the kingdom of Lesotho. This shows that when we respond in time to any African crisis, lives and properties can be saved, and the conflict can be resolved earlier. During the uprising in the kingdom of Lesotho, South Africa sent in troops and was able to stop the crisis, stabilise the country, and restore the rightful ruler, thus preventing what would have turned into a civil war. Most of the time, both regional and international bodies play safe in an African crisis till it becomes obvious that lives have been lost in millions, displacement has taken place, or refugees become burdens to neighbouring nations. In some cases, if time is not taken, there will be a spillover of the conflicts. This cycle continues from year to year and decade to decade; time has come when we have to be reasonable enough to know that intervention in the early stage can save us from prolonged conflicts that are no longer needed in the continent.

These conflicts in Africa limit and derail our supposed development and achievements in many areas in Africa. Let us join hands and learn from other continents who have shunned wars and conflict and instead have directed their energy and potentials in moving forward in areas of technology, commerce, infrastructure, and industry.

3. *Mediation.* There is a need for a third party to mediate in order to encourage the parties involved in conflict to start communication. This approach will reduce defensiveness and promote constructive interaction. A mediator of mediators must maintain a neutral position regarding the conflict. There should be no attitude of taking sides if he or she will have success in dealing with the issue at hand.

4. *Dialogue.* We need facilitators who will sit down with those parties involved in conflict to discuss issues in dispute in a constructive and nonconfrontational manner. During this time, a facilitator(s) can create a space for in-depth enquiry. This goal increases mutual understanding without finding an ultimate solution. I believe somebody like Lakhar Ibrahim may be in a better position to give the best solution in this area.

Development of Genuine Democracy and Structures

Most conflicts in Africa have been internal conflicts rather than external—that is to say, conflicts within the nation, not nation-to-nation conflicts. There is indication that the lack of equality, tribalism, nepotism, dictatorship, as well as corruption has been the main cause of most of the internal conflicts ravaging the continent of Africa. We learnt from secondary education government that democracy is 'the government of the people, by the people, and for the people'. However, democracy being practised in many parts of Africa does not match the definition of 'democracy'. Many leaders of many nations in Africa have ruled the lands as their private kingdoms and for the interests of their families, clans, tribes, and political friends.

This has contributed to instability and agitation by the disenfranchised people of different states. It has created conflicts and wars fought within nations and some ongoing ones. If governance becomes good where citizens of the same state have equal opportunity, there will be no idea of separation, which creates conflict and violence. Marginalisation has angered many ethnic blocks; as such, they may decide to fight for redress. Sometimes it seems that it may pay off, but most of the time, it only brings misery to the oppressed and the oppressors themselves, and a whole lot become victims.

The international community and many colonial powers affiliated with Africa must and have to work towards building a genuine democracy and democratic structure in the continent. The help we need from the foreign and international community must be genuine and devoid of colonial mentality of trying to devise a system that allows them to decide for us how to live our lives in terms colonial domination, but rather building democratic structures as they are in their own regions, devoid of tricks and hidden agendas of a re-colonial approach. The idea created by the Christian missionaries in the history of Rwanda and other parts of Africa where the colonial masters made some clan or tribe seem more important than others should be completely out of place in this new dispensation of trying to build a genuine democracy that will thrive.

In the history of Ghana, Songhai, and the Benin Empire, the leaders ruled with righteousness and care and had the people's interests at heart. Genuine democracy ushers in development, innovation, and progress and reduces friction, agitation, and violent conflict that have dominated our history in recent decades after independence. The West hurriedly abandoned Africa, went away, and took their time planning how to control us from afar. They instigate conflict to remove leaders who refuse to dance to their beat. The continued idea of the West to support and tolerate leaders who are undemocratic in nature for their own interest should be discontinued so that Africa can move forward for good. Let there be a government of the people, by the people, and for the people. By the time this nature of democracy begins to function in the continent, we will be able to overcome our odds, making conflict a thing of the past.

CHAPTER 6

Ending or Reducing Corruption in the Continent

Many nations around the world with advanced and genuine democratic principles have managed to reduce corrupt attitudes and practices in government. There are checks and balances and the rule of law that limit and control corruption to a great extent. It is realistic that corruption cannot be completely removed from any system, but it has been limited in many parts of the globe through drastic laws that carry heavy consequences for doing so. In many communist societies in the past and present, the cost to pay for corruption is and was high when apprehended.

In China, when communism was really strong and active, the death penalty and other severe punishments awaited anyone caught in corrupt practices. Even though communism is losing its grip in many parts of the world (including China and Cuba) these days, many government officials are still very cautious in getting involved in corruption. Genuine democratic ideals have a strong way of applying the laws so that those who contravene the law get punished. In the context of the African continent, the absence of genuine democracy and structures as well as solid-based institutions has created room for corruption.

We know that there is corruption in almost every part of the globe, but the levels of corruption differ from country to country.

The continent of Africa is one of the richest places in the world, but also one of the poorest due to the lack of genuine democracy and corruption embedded in the government system. Many African nations are listed amongst the most corrupt countries in world.

Someone may ask, 'What is corruption?' 'Corruption', according to *Oxford English Dictionary*, is 'wrongdoing on the part of an authority or powerful party through means that are illegitimate, immoral, or incompatible with ethical standards'. Corruption often results in patronage and is associated with liberty. This definition might not satisfy all about what corruption is, but it gives us an ample idea what we are talking about here. In Africa, the major corrupt practices are committed by political leaders or those in power. It has crossed boundaries in affecting the whole society, wherein it has become normal to be corrupt. In a situation where you want to act contrary to being moral or ethical, you are seen as a person that doesn't understand what is going on.

Political Corruption

This is the use of power by government officials for illegitimate private gains. An illegal act by an office holder constitutes political corruption only if the act is directly related to official duty and is done under the colour of class or involves trading in influence. Corruption varies in forms, which include bribery, extortion, nepotism, and embezzlement.

Corruption mainly facilitates and encourages criminal enterprise, such as drug trafficking, money laundering, and human trafficking. However, it is not restricted only to these activities. Misuse of government power for other purposes such as repression of political opponents and general police brutality is not considered as political corruption. Neither are illegal acts by private persons or corporations not directly involved with the government. However, there are cases where political corruption gives room for both persons and corporations to abuse the system or become corrupt in their dealings in a given state.

We know that activities that constitute illegal corruption might differ from country to country and depend on the nation or jurisdiction. For instance, some political funding practices that are illegal in one place may be legal in another. It has been discovered that bribery alone worldwide is estimated to be over $1 trillion annually, according to Transparency International. We know that corruption and corrupt practices can't be completely rooted out of the world system of things, but we need to sanitise the minds of mostly those in authority to limit the level of corruption induced into the government systems. Around the globe, Africa has completely become a victim to and become sick of the word 'corruption' because it has derailed the progress and development of the continent. The Western accomplices that support this system in African nations should redress in truth and not only by blowing their trumpet against corrupt African heads of government while they aid and abate them.

Millions of wealth from Africa has made many Western people and states rich and wealthy, while the people of the continent suffer and become ridiculed by the citizens of the West who have benefited from its wealth. We are in part aware of some billions of dollars lodged in Western banks by African political leaders, which are never retrieved by different nations the money belongs to. Muammar Gaddafi of Libya had a series of petrol stations in the West that had gone down the drain since his death. His billions in most of the Western banks have turned to development project money for the West, while Libyans suffer and come back to the West, begging for funds through borrowing again to mortgage their future and those of the future generations to come.

'Kleptocracy' is a term that defines the attitude of most world leaders and government officials today, especially in Africa. This means a ruling by thieves due to unrestrained political corruption. Corruption has become part of every institution in many African nations as well as some other places around the globe; in Africa, it has become epidemic that requires a 'vaccine' to cure. In fact, corruption has become institutionalised in our political systems. Public officers continue to get personal gains to the detriment of the public. Institutions and government policies or processes with bias to some special interests remain active in the system. These behaviours by some in authority have undermined public confidence in those in government. The ethical and moral principles have no longer have a place in the minds and souls of those who rule us.

In Africa, most of the so-called democracy has just turned into a monarchy because of corruption; many ruling presidents after holding power for long prepare their sons, brothers, and clans to take over. Cases abound where the president's choice of minister has to be his daughter, son, cousin, or brother whether he or she can deliver or not. The government of clienteles has become the order of the day. For example, the late president Eyadéma of Togo, after years of ruling, had his son take over. Omar Bongo of Gabon, the only face known by many in Gabon, is gone; and then his son, the late Gaddafi, was busy trying to transfer power to his son before fate caught up with him. Ex-president Mubarak of Egypt was grooming Gamal Mubarak to take over Egypt before the Arab Spring took him by surprise. The former president of Ghana John Kufuor appointed his brother as minister as if there were no other people in Ghana who could be effective in government.

What can we say then about this class of people with a corrupt mindset who lack reformation despite being educated abroad, where the principles of democracy are supposed to run deep in the minds of leaders who can just resign their positions when they defaulted in discharging their duty to the public? I remember former British prime minister Gordon almost crying on television because of his involvement in the misuse of £3,000 in terms of housing. So which African leader would ever feel remorse for billions of dollars looted from the nation's treasury?

This is an example of what we mean by looking at corruption and corrupt practices around the world.

In Nigeria, the so-called largest nation in the continent of Africa, the PDP has hijacked and dominated the Nigerian political system that, in fact, you can't talk of opposition. It has bastardised and corrupted the system of democracy that it has lost its meaning. The political climate in Nigeria has turned sour that it has become the worst place for a decent mind to imagine getting involved in. Nigerian politics have become like a Sicilian clan, filled with terror, deaths, and threats. If you are not ready to shed blood and get corrupt, there is no need for you to dare go near it.

Transparency International

According to Transparency International, an organ of the United Nations that exposes corruption, most of the corrupt countries are in Africa, with scores below 50. Looking at the index, you see that nations with good democratic structures and practise genuine democracy are less corrupt than those deceiving themselves with the term 'democracy'. The 2012 index shows a map of Africa complete with its high level of corruption with only one spot of yellow (South Africa). So who will save us from this disease that has crippled the continent from moving forward in terms of development and progress?

Effects of Corruption on Politics, Administrations, and Institutions

Generally speaking, corruption in politics undermines democracy as well as good governance by flouting or even subverting formal processes. Corruption in elections and the legislature reduces accountability and distorts representation in policymaking. Corruption in the judiciary compromises the rule of law, which leads to abuse of power, and corruption in public administration results in the inefficiency of provision of services. It violates a basic principle of republicanism regarding the centrality of civic virtues. More generally, corruption erodes the institutional capacity of government if procedures are disregarded, resources of government or the people are siphoned off, and public offices are bought and sold. Corruption undermines the legitimacy of government and, in this case, democratic values such as trust and tolerance. In recent times, evidence has shown how high levels of corruption are found amongst high-income democracies. It points out that this can vary significantly depending on the level of accountability of decision makers.

In the context of Africa, this a major bottleneck in the so-called practice of democracy by most nations in the continent. The whole system of democratic principles has been destroyed by political leaderships. Elections in many countries in Africa are marred by irregularities, rigging, intimidation, and violence. The right of the citizens are neglected and thrown to the mud since their votes don't count after selections. Those who head public offices have no respect for ethics and morality. All important institutions that hold and maintain democracy are inefficient and ineffective even where they tend to exist. The police, army, judiciary, etc. lack legitimacy because the citizens have no confidence and trust in them. They serve only the rich, the government, and her cliques. People have given up hope; in fact, this affected the basic structure in a way that there is no plan for progress and development. Each and every person wants to be in government for himself or herself, and nobody thinks of making plans for future generations. Laying foundation for progress and development has eluded most of the nations in the continent of Africa. Nigeria is one of the most corrupt countries in the world despite the high potential that exists there, which if harnessed can be an example for the continent of Africa to move towards development and progress.

In all that we have discussed about political corruption, the nation of Nigeria is a place you can see all the instances given above of what effects corruption has on politics, administrations, and institutions. All the irregularities that are associated with a corrupt system is well and alive there. Who do we leave out in this in Africa—South Africa, Egypt, Sudan, Zimbabwe, Ghana, etc.? There is nowhere in the continent that can be exonerated, though some nations are a little bit better than others in this context.

When it comes to elections, nations like Ghana and others have improved, showing that there is hope for free and fair elections. In the case of Nigeria, the so-called largest democracy in Africa, there is nothing to write home about. It is the worst place in the continent in terms of free and fair elections. This is a do-or-die affair. Election in Nigeria is 'war'. Politicians can do anything to make sure the win since it is about them and not about the governed. They can kill and destroy to make sure they get in there. In fact, it is 'dirty'.

If Africa can learn how to conduct free and fair elections, then we will be on our way to a new future; the people's choice will be elected into office. They will do the work of the people for another chance. The late Ted Kennedy, the people's representative, presented about three hundred bills in the US House before his death. Some of the bills were passed, and they all improved the lives of the ordinary citizens of the state. However, in the continent of Africa, the so-called honourable members of the houses of legislature are a bunch of criminals who don't give a damn about those they represent. Some women politicians in places like Kenya have given the African women and the rest of us hope that women, if given more chances in politics, can do better for the good of the continent. But in Nigeria, count the women out—they are as corrupt as their male counterparts. The disease of corruption in that nation has affected almost everyone, if not all. Even the women, the pride of human society, have become corrupt to a level that can't be seen anywhere in the world in terms of females being corrupt.

Economic Effects of Corruption

Corruption, being what it is, has a negative effect in every area of the society—political, social, economic, etc. When the political, administrative, social, and democratic systems become corrupt, the economy and other areas are also affected. In terms of the effects of corruption on economics, both the private sector and corporate sector are in jeopardy. Businesses suffer hugely, either directly or indirectly, because of corruption rooted in the system. The lack of progress and development in Africa can be attributed to all these. Business communities around the globe sometimes fear to invest in a corrupt system, while others prefer it so that they would have their way and benefit to the detriment of the given state where corruption thrives.

Corruption in the private sector increases the cost of doing business through the price of illicit payments. Management of the private sector pays more in negotiating with corrupt officials, and there is the risk of a breach of contract or agreement. However, some people claim that corruption can reduce costs by cutting bureaucracy, and the availability of bribes can also persuade officials to contrive new rules and delays. This can openly remove costly and lengthy regulations, which is better than covertly allowing them to be bypassed by using bribes. Where corruption inflates the cost of doing business, it also distorts the playing field, shielding firms with connections from competition and thereby sustaining inefficient firms.

This type of immediate scenario plays well in the continent of Africa, where corrupt officials care less about their fatherland.

Patriotic citizens shun this kind of actions because it is to the detriment of the nation in question. The Niger Delta in Nigeria is a victim of Royal Dutch Shell and other oil companies, and its inhabitants have been affected economically by this type of corruption. Their source of living through agriculture and fishing and even their health have been damaged by the corruption between the state and these corporate organisations.

Economically speaking, corruption generates distortions in the public sector by diverting public investments into capital projects where kickbacks and bribery are enormous. In capital projects, it is also not so easy for ordinary people to know how it is being managed or run. Here, the officials have the chance to increase the technical complexity of public sector projects to conceal or pave the way for such dealings, thus further distorting investments. Corruption also reduces compliance to construction, environmental, and other regulations. It also lowers the quality of government services and infrastructure, and as such, this tends to increase pressure on government budgets.

There has been an argument by economists saying that one of the factors behind the difference in 'economic development' in Africa and Asia is that corruption in Africa has mainly taken the form of rent extraction. This causes the resulting financial capital to be transferred or lodged overseas rather than being invested in the home country (hence the stereotypical but often accurate image of African dictators having Swiss bank accounts). I remember that the late Mobutu Sese Seko of Congo moved most of his stolen wealth to Morocco, where he later died. The wealth of Congo laundered into Morocco was never recovered by any government after him. This is how Africa has lost a reasonable amount of wealth, which would have played a vital role in the development of the continent.

In Nigeria, for example, more than $400 billion was stolen from the treasury by Nigerian leaders between 1960 and 1999. According to research carried out by the University of Massachusetts Amherst, researchers estimated that from 1970 to 1996, capital flight from thirty sub-Saharan countries totalled $187 billion, exceeding those nations' external debts. The results, which are expressed in retarded or suppressed development, were been modelled in theory by the economist Mancur Olsen. (See 'political corruption' in *Wikipedia*.) The political instability in Africa has been identified as one of the factors for corrupt behaviour by leaders; this is also coupled with the fact that new governments often confiscate previous governments' corruptly obtained assets in the home country where possible. We only hear that money is confiscated, but it will never be put in use for the public; rather, the new politician will share it amongst themselves. To date, all the money retrieved from the family of the late Sani Abacha was never accounted for. The Nigerian public has never benefited from such an action where it has been carried out; maybe it has happened in other African nations. It is assumed that the confiscation of stolen wealth when discovered is a reason for officials to stash their ill-gotten or stolen wealth abroad, out of reach of any future expropriation. In contrast, Asian administrations such as Suharto's New Order often took a cut on business transactions or provided conditions for development through infrastructure investment as well as law and order.

The question to the African leaders and officials here is, how many foreign government leaders have lodged their wealth, whether stolen or clean, in the continent? Also, why would they be busy stealing more than what they needed to live as a person? The most annoying thing in the Nigerian context is that it has become a culture where a public servant that doesn't steal from the state or the public becomes a dummy, while those who steal our wealth are praised and cheered even by those whose wealth they stole. Most of them are compensated by the stupid society, giving them titles either in the villages or universities. Every man in his right frame of mind who is not morally and ethically bankrupt would agree with me that corruption in Africa has hampered progress and development in many areas of our society. This is like Ebola, which has no cure; we should demand for inventors to design a vaccine that can protect politicians and public officers from having a corrupt mindset.

The word 'corruption', being alive and well in Africa, has made the word 'transparency' a misnomer. The leaders and public officers are involved in deals with Western companies that don't benefit the nations in the long term. The selfish ambition of many political and public officers is also working against the state and citizens of most given states in the continent of Africa. Globalisation becomes an economic disadvantage to Africa since the market was never done on an equal scale. The West can get resources from Africa based on their own prices, while Africans pay more to obtain their needed products from the West. Due to corruption, there is no genuine agreement amongst African leaders; rather, they work only for their self-interest. The lack of a joint stand in having a common ground for the prices of their products continues to benefit the West, while African nations suffer more economically.

Effects of Corruption on the Environment and Social Issues

Most countries in Africa are countries with small per capita incomes, and this is possible because of corruption. Evidence has shown that corruption is common in nations with small average incomes (per capita incomes), who rely more on foreign aid for health services. You will bear with me that many nations in Africa are in this category because of corruption, not necessarily because that the respective nations don't have resources that will raise their standard of living. It has been noted that the political exploitation of foreign funds has been occurring in the past, especially in the sub-Saharan African nations. The World Bank report of 2006 stated that about half of funds donated for health use were never invested into the health sectors or given to those needing medical attention. Instead, they were expanded through counterfeit drugs, thereby siphoning off drugs to the black market and payments to ghost workers.

It has been said that there is a sufficient amount of money for health in developing nations such as those in Africa. Unfortunately, the cash is given to the wrong hands, which leads to political or governmental corruption. This takes away medical attention necessary for the citizens of the given states or regions and is rather directed for personal gain. For instance, Uganda is one of the nations that receive significant funds for health issues, but it is unfortunate that these funds are not rightly used for the healthcare of the people. I happened to see a life programme in Uganda where patients in a local hospital were lying on bare floors instead of beds. Just tell me how the survival of that patient is guaranteed. Meanwhile, some of the government officials can be flown abroad to receive medical treatment. Using the funds given to them to build quality healthcare becomes impossible and difficult because of corruption; instead, the same funds are secretly lodged into foreign accounts of the same people giving you the aid fund to help yourselves. It is unfortunate and embarrassing that this attitude continues to show its ugly face in the continent of Africa.

The existence of corruption in the system facilitates the destruction of the environment. Nations where corruption is high may formally have legislation to protect the environment, but sometimes it cannot really enforce it if officials are or can easily be bribed. The same applies to social rights workers protection and the prevention of unions and child labour. Violation of these laws and rights enables corrupt countries to gain illegitimate economic advantage in the international market.

The Niger Delta area of Nigeria is a good example when it comes to the effects of corruption on the environment. Due to corruption, the oil companies pollute the environment without being held accountable for the damages caused to the local people. Somehow these multinational oil companies know what the law says, but since they can use bribery to get their way, there is no need to take care of the environment. Many public or government officials in the affected area take bribes from the oil companies, and with that, little or nothing can be said or done about environmental degradation. The last time industrial waste from Europe was dumped in the Ivory Coast, it caused harm to the environment, people, and wildlife. It was possible because of corruption in the system. Once the corrupt officers take their money, to hell with the environment, the laws, and the people affected by it.

According to Amartya Sen, a one-time Nobel Prize winner and economist, 'There is no such thing as an apolitical food problem.' While drought and other naturally occurring events may trigger famine conditions, it is government action or inaction that determines its severity and often even whether or not a famine will occur. Governments with strong tendencies towards kleptocracy can undermine food security even when harvests are good. Officials often steal state property. In Bihar in India, more than 80 per cent of the subsidised food aid to the poor is stolen by corrupt officials. Similarly, food aid is often robbed at gunpoint by governments, criminals, and warlords alike and sold for profit. The twentieth century is full of many examples of governments undermining the food security of their own nations—sometimes intentionally.

This is not something common to India alone; many nations in Africa where drug supplies for HIV/AIDS and other ailments always find their way in the black markets through illicit activities of corrupt government and public health workers. During the Biafra-Nigerian Civil War, cornmeal given by the United Nations for malnourished children was sold in the open market. All these are actions of corrupt public officials. In a well-democratic setting, these actions are limited or nonexistent because the people know what the consequences are if apprehended. The rule of judiciary institutions is there to take care of those who abuse the law, but in the case of most African nations, it is a 'free for all' behaviour, for the law is silent.

Other Areas Where Corruption
Affects the Continent of Africa

Though we have looked at some areas where corruption affects the development and progress of the nations of Africa, there are still many other areas that will be treated here collectively. In chapter 3 of this book, the issue of institutions was analysed based on facts.

We know an efficient and effective institution can help gear any given nation forward, but where the institutions are not well structured and founded, things go wrong. In the continent of Africa, many institutions lack credibility due to corruption that is rooted in the system. The effects of corruption on these institutions make it even more easy for corrupt officials and government leaders to escape punishment when found wanting in discharging their duties. Corruption covers the failures and abuse of office by those in leadership and other public officers. In this context, most corrupt leaders are left alone or exonerated if at any time indicted for wrongdoing.

In fact, I am not here to paint Africa black as if it is the only place in the world that corruption exists; it is not. However, I am concerned because the issue of corruption has played a big role in limiting our progress and development as a people, individually and collectively. This incurable disease has derailed the entire continent from its move forward, development, and innovation in all walks of life. You may not agree with me. But take your time and ask yourself if there are elements of truth or facts in what I am saying. Then you will not be far from the truth.

Corruption is not specific to only developing, poor, and transition countries. Cases of bribery and other forms of corruption exist in all possible fields. It is discovered that in the US, under-the-table payments are made to reputed surgeons by patients attempting to be on top of the lists of forthcoming surgeries. This is happening in one of the advanced nations in the world. But the fact remains that when caught, the people involved—both surgeons and patients—will automatically be punished. That means that there are consequences for doing something illegal. In terms of Africa and other developing nations, nothing will be done. Suppliers to the automotive industries paid bribes in order to sell low-quality connectors used, for example, in safety equipment such as airbags.

Many wealthy parents paid contributions to social and cultural funds of prestigious universities in exchange for their children's acceptance into the school. Bribes are paid to obtain diplomas. Financial and other advantages are granted to unionists by members of the executive board of manufacturing companies in exchange for employer-friendly positions, votes, etc. There are countless examples of manifestations of corruption, and they can present danger to the public institutions and discredit a lot of essential institutions and social relationships.

Nigeria is a good example of many of these awful corrupt practices that have hampered development and progress. Poor families today cannot send their children to quality schools or universities since education now is the highest bidder gets through. The idea after a JAMB examination, then internal university exams have promoted corruption, where only those whose parents can pay the bribes get admitted into the colleges of higher learning or universities. The issue of merits is dead; only cash can talk. These have led a lot of young women into prostitution in order to achieve their dreams of getting an education. Admission officers and vice-chancellors of higher institutions receive sex or money in exchange for admission. It is embarrassing and disheartening that even all the mosques and churches in and around all corners of the streets in Nigeria and other African nations don't make a difference in building quality morals and ethical attitudes in public officers. In fact, I can't go further because this book won't be able to cover it if I intend to discuss it all.

Worldwide, corruption can affect areas like sports activities, including the players, medical and laboratory staff involved in antidoping controls, and members of national sports federations and international committees deciding about the allocation of contracts and competition venues. We know how long it took to discover that Lance Armstrong of the USA used performance-enhancing drugs. After this was discovered, many heads rolled in sports in terms of doping corruption in the cycling world and athletics.

Sepp Blatter and members of the world football governing body, FIFA, were rocked last 2015 with corruption charges. In fact, many heads rolled when the sledgehammer of justice hit the entire body. In African football, Issa Hayatou has become another name for the Confederation of African Football (CAF). He is now just like his fellow African political dictators we have known all our lives. He is not there because there is no other African who can head the organisation, but he has remained as a result of corruption. So what happens when he dies? Does that mean that there will be no other person to lead CAF? Anyway, that is what it looks like since he is there like Mugabe.

In terms of nonprofit and nongovernmental organisations as well as religious organisations, it has become evident that they have also become infected with this disease of corruption. In recent years, people have looked into these organisations and have discovered a high level of corruption in them. Some charity funds have made their leaders affluent where the resources and finances were really collected for the poor. Religious bodies that were fathers of social systems in history have turned around to extort money from their followers. Most of the pastors have become the richest people in the world, whereas the followers have become victims of the new form of 'indulgence' pay money—get blessed, and your sins are forgiven you. The church is a place of support and truth, said the apostle Paul in the Bible. But if the church has turned into a place of robbery and lies, then we are in damn trouble. Helps us, O God, and also save us from those who say they love you.

Religious organisations and charity organisations should be good examples to others rather than being corrupt just like other organs of the government. Christ warned people in the temple who were selling items with wrong measures and weights. He drove out of the temple the money changers who were cheating people. He set a good example for those who said they would follow him. However, what we get today from religious organisations are moral bankruptcy, corruption, and stealing, which are against the Messiah's will for us. Let us abhor corruption by turning a new leaf.

We all know that there is a difference between public and private sector corruption, and sometimes it appears rather artificial. Some countries have taken anticorruption initiatives to curb corruption, but sometimes there are loopholes that allow culprits to escape punishment. The Nigerian anticorruption agent Economic and Financial Crimes Commission (EFCC), initiated under former president Obasanjo, was a good idea. But it became a political witch-hunt machine against the opposition. It is what a country like Nigeria really needed to impede or limit corruption in its system in order to move the country forward. Unfortunately, after a while, the agent became like other institutions and agents in Nigeria that are inefficient and ineffective like a toothless bulldog. The agent itself became corrupted, being manipulated by the party in power. So instead of serving the public interest, which is highly needed, it served the same people abusing our democratic set-up. What a pity for the citizens of the nation. There are many of these examples in many nations of Africa.

It is high time well-patriotic Africans came up with anticorruption ideas and plans to reduce and tackle corruption in our system if we wish and hope to move forward just like other continents around the globe. It is indicated that over $187 billion have been stashed out in foreign bank accounts by African political and public office holders. However, this is just little of the much that is stolen. The cash stashed overseas by people like Gadaffi, Mubarak, Mobutu, Omar Bongo, Paul Biya, Abacha, Obasanjo, Goodluck, and their political aides is well above $700 billion. Only Nigerian political and public officers since 1960 have stolen over $400 billion from Nigerians. This is only cash that has been traceable by a study done in the USA; other assets such as cars and houses are not included.

In fact, citizens should pressure governments to implement laws that will hang any African leader or public officer caught stealing the people's money for his or her own use. Let it be like in then communist China. Get corrupt and risk being hanged. This can serve as a deterrent to those greedy and overambitious office holders in the continent of Africa.

There is a great need for continental African leaders and public officers to learn how to be humane, moral, and ethical in ruling over their citizens, if not subjects. For now, they are more hostile to us than the occupiers—I mean the colonial masters. The colonial fathers were dealing with the people they really didn't have anything in common with and as such treated Africans harshly and abusively. But the worst thing in life is when your present enemy is the member of your family. Those who steal our wealth and at the same time chastise us with guns and whips are our own brothers and sisters in uniform and our bosses that give us mandates to do so. So when you are being chased from the house, what can you do, and where can you run to? The selfish and greedy ambitions in our so-called African leaders have derailed our progress with corruption and bad leadership with no end in sight.

The Indian thinker Roy said, 'What Africa lost in natural disaster, she got in political disaster.' Before, I didn't really believe him, but now the handwriting on the wall has proven that it is true. Our Mother Africa is weeping, groaning, and dying because of our wicked, greedy, and corrupt leaders. Please, brothers and sisters of Africa, let the citizens rise against these leaders and demand that they give us freedom or death. When we rise up against them, they will all run away instead of us running away because of them. The Ben Alis, Gaddafis, Mubaraks, Mobutus, and Idi Amins have shown us that the power of the people is great—power to the people.

Types of Corruption

Bribery

It is good that you, as a reader, understand what bribery is because you can be a giver or a receiver of it in one way or another. In fact, it is possible the law of a given state should look at what measure should be taken regarding both parties depending on the circumstances. A giver may be forced to give bribes or may be constrained or forced to do so, or he can initiate it; in this case, the law of the state should weigh in.

Bribe is a payment given to a government official in exchange of his use of official powers. It requires two participants—that is to say, one to give the bribe and one to take it. Either may initiate the corrupt offering; for instance, a customs official may demand bribes to allow or disallow certain goods, or a smuggler might offer bribes in order to gain passage. In many countries like the continental African nations, this is mostly a usual practice by customs and other security agents. This also increases the prices of commodities since a businessman will add up his expenses on the price of the products. The culture of corruption extends to every aspects of public life, thereby making it extremely difficult for an individual to stay in business without resorting to bribery. Public officials may still demand bribes to do work they are already paid for. Every public officer receives his or her salary from the institution or government agents that employs him or her, so by taking bribe, they contravene the ethics of public service. They also may demand bribes in order to bypass laws and regulations. Furthermore, they use bribery for their private financial gains. In most, if not all, of the nations of Africa and beyond, many have paid bribes at one time or another to obtain something or let something be done for him or her.

However, you have to bear with some of them due to the circumstances surrounding them. For example, many police take bribes because the state doesn't pay them a reasonable salary that can solve their individual problems. Due to this, they tend to take bribes in order to survive. In places like Nigeria, you can always bear with the police because some of them are living in very disgusting places. Teachers in Nigeria are even worse to talk about since some of them are not paid salaries for three months. So in this case, the man needs to take bribes from students in order to survive too. Most of these public servants also have families like every other person. If you work and can't provide for your family because of the government's mismanagement, corruption, and lack of fulfilling their responsibilities to the citizens, then the citizens may opt for another means to survive. It becomes a chain reaction; the society has become corrupt due to bad governance and the lack of efficient and effective institutions.

Patronage

This isn't a bad word to use, but when it comes to corruption, it has done a lot of damage to our society. It is an unequal social treatment whereby favours are granted from a higher person to a lower person in exchange for service, support, or trust. Many political appointments are done based on patronage. Regarding the selection of recruits in the military, police, and other government agencies, it should be on merit rather than patronage. But sometimes the opposite is the case. Some cases of patronage are well deserved, while some are not. Patronage can also refer to favouring supporters, for example, with government employment. This may be legitimate when a newly elected government changes the top officials in the administration in order to effectively implement its policy.

In terms of corruption, it denotes negativity because it has granted unnecessary favours to people not qualified enough to handle some offices, such as certain ministries, commissions, or institutions. In many countries in Africa, patronage has damaged our different nations because it has made life difficult for the entire society. In fact, patronage becomes corruption when this means putting incompetent persons in place of more competent ones as a payment for supporting the regime in power.

Since most nations in Africa are developing and recently practising democracy, this has become a big problem and derailment in building a strong society and institutions. Our government officials are being selected based on loyalty and party patronage rather than on abilities. They always put square pegs in round holes, which don't fit. Most of the time, Nigeria typically exemplifies this problem in Africa, though not alone.

Other examples also abound in other developing nations in the Middle East, where selections are made based on party affiliation and patronage. During the time of Saddam Hussein of Iraq, the Ba'th Party associates were always selected for posts. (Other examples include in Syria, the Ba'th Party, Alawite Muslims, etc.; in Nigeria, the PDP; in Ghana, the New Patriotic Party (NPP); in South Africa, the African National Congress (ANC).)

Trading Influence

Many can see this as what we call 'peddling influence', where a person can be selling his or her influence over a decision-making process to benefit a third party, which can even be a person or an institution. The difference between this and bribery is that there is a trilateral relation involved. Looking at this legally, the role of the third party, who is the target of influence, does not really matter, though he or she can be an access in some instances. It can be difficult to make distinctions between trading influence as a corruption practices and other forms of extreme and some loosely regulated lobbying where, for example, decision makers can freely 'sell their vote', decision power, or influence to those lobbyists who offer the highest compensation.

Trading influence is a corruption practice that is not known to the public due to how it operates because in some cases, it might not be detrimental to the citizens. In the West, trading influence has become such a problem that many are calling for international convention to criminalise it. Willeke Stuarlen of the University of Enschede in the Netherlands has voiced his concern about this type of corruption in the developed democracies where influences are been traded.

A recent case occurred where the Duchess of York, Sarah Ferguson, was promising access to her ex-husband, Prince Andrew, who serves as a quasi-official trade envoy for Great Britain to rich businessmen. This is an example of such clear cases in which a person promises to exert improper influence over the decision-making process of a public official in return for undue advantage. Other examples of trading influence occurred in France involving former French president Nicolas Sarkozy and the L'Oreal heiress Liliane Bettencourt for the public financing of his presidential campaign.

Most of us know that corruption is more or less everywhere, but the difference is in the level of corruption and the prize to pay when caught. In many nations in the continent of Africa, many who become indicted, if possible, never pay any price for their crimes. In the other parts of the globe, those involved in corruption always suffer when caught. And sometimes it does not matter how long. The influence trading has on most countries in Africa has derailed goodwill and, in many cases, negatively affected projects that benefit the common people. Trading influence finds its way in every institution in Africa.

Corrupt officials and criminals have been exonerated through these corrupt practices. Stronger and more effective, efficient, and democratic values limit and fight this type of corruption because they don't compromise it.

Nepotism and Cronyism

This is a type of corruption where favouritism is granted in politics, organisations, and religious bodies to relatives or close friends (cronies). It originated from the assigning of nephews to cardinal positions by Catholic popes and bishops. However, in 1769, Pope Innocent X ended it in the Catholic Church. It is also mostly found in the fields of politics, entertainment, business, and religion. At times, nepotism is a means of continuity of a dynasty or leadership. It creates room for people to attain positions they are not qualified for in an inappropriate manner. Favouritism to relatives or personal friends (cronyism) is for illegitimate private gain. This may be combined with bribery. For instance, demanding that a business should employ a relative of an official controlling regulations will affect the business. The most extreme case is when an entire state is inherited, as in North Korea or places like Syria, Gabon, Togo, and Libya. This sort of corruptions has also taken place in places like Nigeria and Ghana. Many ministers in the Nigerian government, both in the past and present, have on many occasions been made ministers when people with better qualifications and abilities were left out.

Heads of important institutions have handed down positions to mediocre individuals because of a personal or tribal relationship, leaving out those who could do better and are more qualified for the positions.

This has been part of the problem we have in Africa that has limited our development. Unless this type of corruption is looked into and reduced in our system, then the case will remain from generation to generation without any way out. This is why many of our institutions are not living up to the standard they were designed for and therefore hampering the progress that we need. The case of nepotism is alive and well in the present government of Nigeria; the government in power came in with the slogan 'Change', but it has become worse than before.

President Muhammadu Buhari said he is a born-again 'Democrat' to champion change in Nigeria. Unfortunately, Buhari is heading the worst nepotistic government in Nigerian history. He came with the agenda of the Hausa-Fulani leader Usman dan Fodio as well as Ahmadu Bello, who believed only in the politics of nephew, otherwise known as nepotism. Buhari sees other Nigerian states as subjects of the Hausa-Fulani, whereas appointments he's made has revolved around the Hausa-Fulani interest. The Muslim race of the Hausa-Fulani is alive and well in the administration of Buhari.

He lied to the nation and the world when he said in his inaugural speech, 'I belong to nobody, and I belong to everyone.' He used pure lies to usher himself in with the great support he received from his Muslim brother former president Barack Obama, who helped him to take over. Buhari said to an international audience that he would not treat those who gave a 5 per cent vote and those who gave a 95 per cent vote the same way. I thought the world and so-called human rights advocates could see the danger coming to Nigeria. However, if the interest of the West is served, damn who is there and what opinion he holds and what his agenda is for the Nigerian nation. The monster Islamic barbarism has played well in the life of Buhari, who has used the Nigerian state apparatus to massacre Nigerians, mostly Igbos, Middle Belters, and no Hausa-Fulani since he came to power in 2015.

I curse the day Barack Obama and John Kerry got involved in the Nigerian elections. The outcome has become the doom for the nation and has dragged us backwards after the progress we made under the administrations of Jonathan, Obasanjo, and the late Yar'Adua.

Nepotism is practised in most African states, and it is rather unfortunate that most of us condone it when it serves our interest and those of our tribes and a few gullible groups like the Yorubas, who cry foul when the status quo doesn't favour them. The need to an end to nepotism is necessary because it breeds backwardness in the nation.

Election Fraud

This means illegal interference in an election process of any sort, especially that of a state or government. When acts of fraud are committed during an election, it always affects the counts and the general results of the electoral process. It can bring about an increase or decrease, depending on what the perpetrators want to achieve. Election fraud can increase the vote share of the favoured candidate and depress or decrease the vote share of the rival candidates or both. There is also 'voters fraud'; this is a mechanism employed to illegally manipulate voters' registration or the register itself or the idea of intimidation at the polls or improper vote counting.

Election fraud is not a new thing to people in the continent of Africa. Election fraud is one of the corrupt ways that African political leaders have used to maintain their grip on power. Because of election fraud, the principle of democracy and election of 'one man, one vote' has been defeated or is rather dead as far as the continent is concerned. In fact, in many countries in Africa, the so-called election is dead; but we have selection where the power brokers do whatever to put who they want in office rather than elect. Many in the continent have no interest in politics and elections because of the way it has been rubbished as a means of selecting the people's choice.

For example, I myself have neither registered or voted in any election in my country, Nigeria, since 1993 because my vote doesn't count due to the illegitimacy employed in the system of elections in the country. I am quite sure that I am not the only person who has chosen not to participate due to the irregularity in every election, be it local, state, or federal.

Many elections in Africa are now a do-or-die affair because the people fighting to be elected are not going there for your interest, so they employ every criminal means to be selected. The democratic principles of election is not respected in many nations in Africa, and that is why we still have presidents staying in office for twenty to thirty years and still want to remain there. In fact, election fraud and malpractice have derailed Africa, killed its hopes and aspirations, and made nonsense of the word 'election'. How can people such as Mugabe, Omar al-Bashir, Paul Biya, and others remain in power if real elections are done in these places with the people's clear discontent about these fellows? In fact, African nations are in a monarchy, not a democracy.

Elected people in offices behave well for the sake of another election or the possibility of moving onto a higher echelon of government. But in the continent of Africa, the election idea has made election a thing only for the advanced world or nations who understand what an election is. Let us join hands to make election reforms around Africa so that the word 'election' will have real meaning in the lives of the people. This is in order to choose leaders who will lead us to develop, progress, and move forward as opposed to rulers who will rule us with iron fists, milk our money, and crush our hopes and aspirations.

However, Uhuru Kenyatta of Kenya has proven that election results can be respected. This is also true of former president Jonathan, who conceded the election to the opposition even though he was the incumbent. When Uhuru won the last election in 2017, Odinga and his groups cried foul. The Kenyan Supreme Court annulled the election, and Uhuru accepted the decision of the court—a rare thing to see in the African continent. There was another election, and Uhuru Kenyetta still emerged as the winner, which was fantastic to witness in the continent. These types of stories and changes are what we need in the continent to strengthen democracy and give people hope that the sun can still rise in Africa.

A credible election can reduce election fraud and produce quality leaders, knowing that the people can speak with their votes, thereby bringing the change we need.

Embezzlement

This type of corruption runs deep in the public sector, private sector, government, and even in homes. Embezzlement is an act of dishonestly and secretly withholding assets for the purpose of conversion (theft or stealing of such assets by one or more persons or individuals to whom such assets have been entrusted to be held or used for other purposes). It is also seen as a kind of financial fraud. For example, a financial advisor could embezzle funds from investors, or a person could embezzle funds from his or her spouse. We saw the case of Madoff of the United States, who is now serving a life sentence for this. Embezzlement may range from the very minute in nature, involving a small amount, to the immense, involving large sums and sophisticated schemes. Embezzlement is often than not performed in a premeditated manner. It becomes political when it involves public money taken by a public official for use by anyone not specified by the public. It is the personal use of the government that is entrusted with finances and resources.

In the United States and many developed democracies, embezzlement is a serious offence that is punishable under the law of the state. Politicians and public office workers have ruined their careers because they were involved in embezzlement of government or public funds designed for use in other areas. However, it is sad and unfortunate that in many nations in Africa, this is not seen in the eyes of government or public officials as a crime and a form of corruption as well. You become ridiculed in many African nations when you abhor this corrupt attitude. The degree to which African leaders and public officials embezzle our funds and resources has reached an alarming rate that something has to been done to checkmate this before most of the countries become bankrupt.

Guilty, guilty, and guilty I pronounce our political leaders for their attitude, nature, and high degree of embezzlement of our resources to the magnitude that has never been seen in any part of the world. People of the Philippines and the world screamed because of late president Marcos's corruption and embezzlement, but that is a child's play compared with the continent of Africa. Nigerian leaders and public officials rank first in this attitude of corruption. The wealth of the nation has been hijacked by a few political elites and their cronies, while the rest of the population eat from the dustbin. Money made for people's pensions are completely embezzled by one man, and he still walks away free. Fareed Zakaria of CNN's *GPS* said that about $300 million of the Nigerian oil money has been stolen by our public and government officials between 1999 and 2006. Research by the University of Massachusetts puts that at $400 million.

All these stolen and embezzled money is needed to fix our country's dilapidated networks of roads and airports and to build our own airline, infrastructures, and industries that can employ our children after studies. Our educational system and many other institutions are broken. You can't go to health sectors since you don't have medicine or equipment that can diagnose simple sicknesses. This is the case not only in Nigeria, but also almost everywhere in the continent. Our resources and wealth have been lodged in foreign accounts, while nations continue to be indebted to the same West that have our money in their different banks. Let us rise up and say no to these Shylocks who call themselves leaders in Africa. Time has come to call for a revolution against the public and government officials who steal our money. Let there be African Spring!

Embezzlement as corruption has derailed and killed the nations of Africa. Our money has been stolen by those who are supposed to be its custodians, who only keep it for themselves and their immediate families. The type of embezzlement we are talking about is not in local currency, but in dollars, pounds, and euros. They invest our money outside Africa while the continent needs investment in their different nations to absorb the citizens graduating out of schools and higher institutions of learning. Former president Zuma was alleged to have embezzled public funds to the tune of $20 million. This money can change the face of Soweto, which is in the state it was during the apartheid regime. Who amongst the African leaders can be exonerated from this crime? The answer is yet to come because even the encouragement by Mo Ibrahim to move them to good governance through his foundation has not yielded any fruit. He promised to give $1 million to any African president who behaves himself in government, willing to retire when his term of office is completed without causing any fracas. Unfortunately, it has only been once that someone has merited that award. This shows the state of affairs in the continent. In fact, we need serious education in order to inform our population of the effects of this group of corrupt leaders and public officials. To my own understanding, many of the civil societies in Africa don't know much about the constitution, their rights, and the obligations of the government to them, both local and federal.

Religious organisations are not left out in this type of corrupt practices of embezzling public funds. This group that would have been the purest in serving the people have also joined the bad eggs in society. Church money is now run by pastors, their families, and their closest friends, while members are kept in the dark about their contributed funds. In fact, the African church leaders are no different from their political counterparts. Most of them now align themselves with corrupt governments for their own benefit. Their duty to warn and direct the leaders has been abandoned and neglected because of their illicit collaborations.

Kickbacks

A kickback is an official's share of misappropriated funds allocated from his or her organisation or an organisation involved in corrupt bidding. For example, assuming a politician is in charge of choosing how to spend some public funds. He can give a contract to a company that is not the best bidder or allocate more than the designated funds. In this case, the community benefits; and in exchange for betraying the public, the official receives a kickback payment, which is a portion of the sum the company received. This sum itself may be all or portion of the difference between the actual (inflated) payment to the company and the lower market-based price that would have been paid had the bidding been done in the correct manner or been competitive.

This can also take place in the judicial system; a judge can receive portion of the profits that a business makes in exchange for his judicial decisions. The case between a company and a community may be in terms of pollution from the company that affects the community in a negative way. In fact, kickbacks as a type of corruption is not limited to government officials; any situation in which people are entrusted to spend funds that do not belong to them are susceptible to this kickback.

This type of corruption has made African infrastructure the worst in the world. Our roads are half-baked construction. Companies that can deliver goods or services are put out to tender because they refuse to give kickbacks or agree to do half-done jobs. The infrastructures are completely in a bad state because government and public officials neglect the interest of the people and pursue only their own interests and that of their cronies, somehow partners in crime. Projects that should be made durable to benefit the state and citizens have been done in haphazard ways because the officials in charge have compromised the projects because of kickbacks.

For example, the Ajaokuta Steel project of Nigeria has remained nonproductive because of this bad and corrupt attitude by both past and present Nigerian government and public officials in charge. However, one of those government leaders and friends has converted it to their own through privatisation. South Korea is what it is today through her investment in the steel industry; but ours has been derailed because of kickbacks, embezzlement, and other types of corrupt practices that have limited us from developing, advancing, and moving forward like many other continents.

This book cannot cover all the issues of corruption as they concern the African continent, but it can serve as a little conscious awakening to our people and others who might be completely uninformed about what is going on in and around them. Our government and public officials have taken undue advantage of the people they are supposed to protect and care for. We know there is corruption in every part of the world, but our own corruption has been the reason behind our not moving forward as a people. It is of great concern that we find a way to limit and reduce corruption embedded in the African political system. When we can tackle this problem and bring it under control to reduce and limit it to the lowest point possible, then our progress and development will manifest like the rising sun. One may ask why corruption has become a well-accepted norm in Africa.

Reason for Corruption in Africa

Weak Democratic Structures and Institutions

The presence of a weak democratic structure and the lack of strong institutions have encouraged the growth of corruption and bad governance, which has led to the collapse of ethics and moral standards. This has made it easy for corruption to thrive in most nations in the continent. In fact, years after independence, it seemed like the future of every African nation was bright because of the then zeal amongst leaders who had a patriotic spirit to lead. The patriotic spirit was so high that many Africans were hoping for better times to come. However, that hope began to dwindle when many of those leaders began to turn into dictators. Due to this government, corruption stepped in and took over.

When the highest echelon of the governments takes advantage of corruption or embezzlement of the state's treasury, it is sometimes referred to as 'neologism kleptocracy'. Members of the governing class or government can take advantage of the natural resources (e.g. oil, diamond, or cobalt in a few prominent cases or state-owned productive industries). A number of governments in Africa have enriched themselves via foreign aid, which is spent on showy buildings and armaments.

The degree of many corrupt dictators in the continent of Africa has typically resulted in many years of general hardships and suffering for the vast majority of the citizens, as civil society and the rule of law disintegrate, leaving the populace with difficulties and no hope. This has become the story of many African nations that have remained downtrodden by the actions of their corrupt leaders and public officials. A typical or classical example can been seen in the late Congo president Marshal Mobutu Sese Seko's corrupt and exploitative regime. He ruled the Democratic Republic of the Congo from 1965 to 1997, where misused the country's resources and wealth, leaving the nation in a complete state of anarchy from then till now. It is believed that the use of the word 'kleptocracy' gained popularity largely in response to a need to accurately explain the attitude of the Mobutu regime to corruption.

Another example is in Nigeria under the rule of the late general Sani Abacha. He was the de facto president of Nigeria from 1993 until his death in 1998. He is reputed to have stolen the sum of up to $4 billion. To some Westerners, he and his family are always mentioned in the Nigerian 419 letter scams, claiming to offer vast fortunes for 'help' in laundering his stolen fortunes, which in reality turned out not to be true. More than $400 billion has been stolen from the treasury of Nigeria by their leaders between 1960 and 1999 and $300 million between 1999 and 2006.

Can you imagine this kind of wealth in foreign banks? Only little of the amount the West and their African accomplices were able to let us know. So what of the rest of African nations where this group of dictators and allies are still in power and continue to steal our resources and wealth and lodge them into foreign Western accounts?

Imagine how good and productive it would be for our society if this kind of money were invested in the continent of Africa. But these criminals prefer to launder this money away from Africa, where others make good and proper use of it for investment and the development of their individual nations. Most of the time, African nations will still borrow back their own wealth with interest. This has damaged our continent, limiting its improvement and development at all fronts. Our health sectors, educational system, and infrastructures are nothing to write home about due to lack of maintenance, improvement, design, and establishment of new ones for future generations.

The state of affairs in each and every nation in Africa remains the same—dilapidated institutions, poor networks of roads and railways, and no airlines of their own. In short, I can't go further because you can name it. The leaders and public officials can only talk the good talk but never work the work that we can see and benefit from. It is like a curse was put upon them—that you never put to good use the resources and wealth you have. Due to their corrupt practices, the rule of law, checks and balances, and the judiciary become ineffective. The laws to limit and arraign culprits become weak; the immunity clause becomes the law that operates well and one that is well and alive in many nations in Africa. This is allowed in order to protect those who are destroying our lives and the entire society through corruption. The African continent is the only place in the new world that even criminals in government are immune from prosecution. They become above the law, while the rest of us lie in wait to be cut off at any time we go to the streets to voice our concerns. Our sons, daughters, and the pregnant drown in the high seas and shores of Europe in search of food and a better life; meanwhile, a better life is in Africa, but it has been mortgaged by a few political elites and their cronies. Though death is taking them out one after the other, the new generation has taken over where their fathers and friends left off.

So the question is, do we sit and look, or do we stand up and fight for our rights? Let us listen to Bob Marley and rise up and fight for our rights. The failure of institutions and the fear of death in the hands of the political leaders have encouraged corruption in our system. The idea that Negroes are afraid of revolution may have worked well to the advantage of the group of criminals called African leaders. Someone who steals from his own family is the worst criminal in life. Also, the lack of education and informed people has also helped where objective judgement is lacking. This has made many to look at things with a tribal sentiment and inclination instead of in an objective and genuine manner for the benefit of all.

Can We Oppose Corruption?

It is possible for any genuine leadership that is ethically and morally bound to work to oppose and limit corruption in the system. Stronger institutions and stringent laws can work together with the masses to stand against corruption and those who practise it. I remember in 1985 when General Muhammadu Buhari and General Tunde Idiagbon took over in Nigeria from the then-acclaimed corrupt civilian government. I say this because what we called 'corruption' then in Nigeria was only child's play compared with what we have witnessed in this country since that time. Idiagbon's military government came to sanitise the system, killing corruption in all levels of the society. It was unfortunate that government was short-lived due to those who hated the genuine system and who were at odds with what that government wanted for the nation—to bring sanity in all spheres of the society. In fact, the death of that regime took Nigeria back to corruption without limitation. There was a clear indication that, that government would have remedied and limited corruption in the Nigerian system, which would serve as an example to many African nations.

However, it is also sad to see that the architect of that regime has found his way back to the system. Unfortunately, President Muhammadu Buhari is now heading another government in Nigeria where corruption, nepotism, ethnicity, and corruption reign. He promised to fight corruption then, but he is aiding and abetting corruption today. He does not practise what he preached. He criticised medical tourism but became the father and head of medical tourism, spending more than three months in a UK hospital. Meanwhile, billions of naira were voted in his government for Aso Rock Medical Center. What a tragedy to the nation.

Also, Jerry J. Rawlings did a similar thing in Ghana, which in a way has benefited the country for some period of time—reducing corruption in almost every sector of society. However, since the time of then president John Kufuor, the ugly corrupt head of corruption is manifesting again in Ghana.

Strong leadership and a strong, efficient, and effective institution willing to sanitise a nation for the interest of the people can oppose and stand against corruption with all available tools. Mobile telecommunications and radio broadcasting, including all newly developed ICT services, can help fight and oppose corruption, especially in developing nations like ours in Africa, where other forms of communications are limited. For example, in Lagos, the largest city in Nigeria, a mobile telephone video captured how a police officer abused a street vendor for not giving him fish to drink his beer. Can you imagine that—an officer on duty drinking beer in a public place? Many incidents like this occur daily in Nigeria without anybody capturing it, but I hope this will not be swept under the rug like the others. That is the power technology has given us today—to at least let the outside world see the type of corrupt and undemocratic state we are living in, in Africa.

The Internet and video phones have been making changes in recent years around the globe. The light of cameras imprisoned the oppressors, as Martin Luther King Jr. said. So we need to apply it more against the oppressors and corrupt powers in Africa and other developing regions in the world. High-tech telephones also captured how hopeless, corrupt, and racist some black South African police were as they dragged to death their own African brother, whom they tied to the back of a police cab.

We have to begin organising African-integrated anticorruption bureaus just as it exists in India to fight and oppose corruption in our continent. Let us stop alienating ourselves from one another since our problems seem similar. We can join forces against all forms of corruption in government and our political system, just as we joined hands in fighting foreign occupation in Africa to gain our so-called independence. Europe has shown us an example. In the 1990s, initiatives were taken at an international level by the European community—the Council of Europe and the Organisation for Economic Co-operation and Development (OECD)—to put a ban on corruption. In 1996, the Committee of Ministers of the Council of Europe, for example, adopted a comprehensive programme of action against corruption and subsequently issued a series of anticorruption standard-setting instruments.

We also need this kind of approach in Africa to checkmate the level of corruption going on in our system. We also need to call the international community to action. For instance, the Western banks, financial institutions, and governments that allow these corrupt leaders and public officers in Africa to launder our state resources into them should refuse or hand the money back to the people through investing it directly in projects for the masses rather than borrowing it back to us with interest, like they have been doing in the past. In fact, they have to help us because they know where our money is in the West. It will serve Africa right if this kind of method is applied by organisations such as AU, OAU, PIDA, and even more in every nation in the continent; checkmating corruption in all its forms can remedy and reduce corruption in Africa.

The hope for progress, innovation, development, and forward movement lies in our hands. We need not necessarily wait on the West again to help us achieve our desired goals. We have to reach a consensus, adopt the laws, and ask them to help us control, search for, and return our funds stolen by both past and present leaders and public officials. When these conventions and strong laws are implemented in different states and nations in Africa, it can help us address all forms of corruption, involving the public sector, private sector, financial institutions, and governments. Whether they are domestic or transnational, it is highly important that these kinds of laws are adopted, implemented, and respected by all.

Examples Our Leaders Should Follow

The people of Africa tend to present themselves as one of the most religious people in the world. Most of the time, they do behave like they are really committed to God—be it as followers of Islam, Christianity, or other belief systems. In fact, this belief idea is not reflected in the way our leaders and public officials handle the citizens and the affairs of each African nation. This work is not about religion or beliefs, but because of the fact that we claim to be more in tune with God than other people around the globe, I am trying to draw this in.

Also, I will not fail to note or mention President John Magufuli of Tanzania, a devout Catholic who has proven himself as a Christian in serving the people and not being corrupt like his fellow African heads of state. Before being a president, he was minister of works, overseeing projects worth billions and trillions of dollars. However, he was not found wanting to enrich himself through corruption like others. Now as president, he has continued in this direction of selfless service as devout believer, serving all in honesty. I pray and believe that he will immortalise his name in the book of life and before the African people as a good example of how a believer should govern his people.

A genuine believer in God is not corrupt and does not encourage, support, or aid corrupt practices. This brings us to the point that while many of our leaders profess the three major faiths, they still do not live according to the expectations of the faiths they profess. Proverbs 29: 2 says that when the righteous rule, the people rejoice; but when the wicked rule, the people suffer. It is clear now to each and every leader and public officer as well as the citizens themselves to embrace this verse in the Scripture and weigh it to ascertain if they are righteous or wicked before the Creator. The continent of Africa has been weeping, crying, and suffering because of bad leadership. This, therefore, shows that the wicked has been ruling and has been greedy and corrupt in all ramifications. They are interested only in their own bellies, tribes, class, cronies, and families. Tens of billions of dollars needed for development, infrastructure, education, health, and other sectors have been diverted overseas by this group of criminal-minded and corrupt leaders who have held African nations hostage, mortgaging the future of younger generations, both now and in the future.

The Western world in recent centuries has cared less about beliefs, religion, and God; but they have produced the best examples of leadership described in the book of Proverbs. It seems that they have been having the righteous as leaders because their people are always rejoicing. They have respect for their citizens, protect them, provide employment, and share and redistribute the wealth of their respective nation states. Their institutions are perfect and well cared for; infrastructures are nothing to toil with no matter which party comes into power. The leaders and public officials in the West have not at any time transferred their country's wealth to Africa for keep in the African banks. So why are ours doing so? This is a question we have to pose to the so-called kleptocrats in Africa, who have ruined the lives of citizens with one of the best abundant God-given resources and wealth of any kind in the world.

The following is just an aside; my main concern here is to draw attention to citizens and leaders of Africa and the rest of the world as well. There was once an African leader who ruled with righteousness, and within his reign, the people rejoiced. We should look back at history when we say that the older generations were uncivilised because we too are civilised now. They lived a life of integrity and honesty; they had respect for human life. They judged fairly and took care of their own. Most never stole what belonged to the people as our leaders are doing today.

In fact, I will share the story of the great man of Africa, *Umar bin Abdul Aziz of Egypt*. The reign of Abdul Aziz in Egypt's history should be a lesson to those who are ruling us now, and those who will rule in the future have to put him in mind and learn from him. Whether you are Muslim or Christian, we tend to show the world that religion is of great importance or plays a significant role in our lives. Then you have to ask yourself if you would have done as Umar bin Abdul Aziz had as a leader.

He proved that we can still have leaders who fear and respect God and rule in righteousness. Good governance entails a lot of things that are of benefit to the people, both to the poor and rich alike. Those who rule with minimal or no corruption improve the lives of their citizens and leave a legacy for the next generation to follow. In the present time, we have seen how Mandela of South Africa and Masire of Botswana left their legacies. These two behaved themselves—they were less corrupt and not accused of abuse of office, and they denied themselves the dictator syndrome. The lives of these leaders and Umar bin Abdul Aziz should be a wake-up call for new political and public officials as well as every one of us who might one day find himself or herself in a position to serve the people.

As a caliph, Umar bin Abdul Aziz ruled within the ninety-one years of the Muslim caliphate. Those who saw him and worked with him gave testimony of his righteous rule. One incident between him and his wife, Fatima, struck me like a bullet. She approach the leader for a discussion. 'Sir', said Fatima, 'will you spare a few moments for me? I want to discuss a private matter with you.' 'Of course,' replied

Abdul Aziz, raising his head from the nation's paper he was reading. 'But please put off the state lamp and light your own lamp as I do not want to burn the state oil for private talk.'

Can you imagine Goodluck Jonathan of Nigeria telling Patience that (or, for that matter, any of the African leaders or public officials such as Jacob Zuma, Robert Mugabe, and John Mahama)? Could they say such a thing to their wives or friends out of concern not to waste the nation's funds? Who amongst the present political and government officials feel concerned about spending state resources for private matters? President Zuma has been accused of spending $20 million in fixing his private home alone. Do not talk of Nigerian politicians, governors, presidents, or ministers who are sharing Nigeria's money in Ghana must go bags in billions. During the wedding of the Nigerian president's daughter, the guests received gold tablets. It is only in Africa where you see this kind of corrupt behaviour of the leaders of the people. They embezzle the people's resources, transferring billions of dollars for their personal use, while the citizens of the nations suffer.

Umar bin Abdul Aziz's reign was described as democratic and as 'rain falling on arid soil'. He transformed the Islamic world—expanding cities, beautifying many places of worship in Medina, and building elaborate infrastructures. He was anxious to improve the welfare of the people he governed. His rule was beneficial to all classes, caring for and improving the lives of not only his family, tribes, clans, or provinces—as those of today do—but also that of everyone else. Abdul Aziz attracted refugees from far places such as Iraq because Iraq then was under the oppressive rule of the then dictator Haif Bin Yussuf. Similarly, many African children have gone on exile in many foreign lands around the world because of wicked, oppressive, and corrupt governments that do not care about their citizens' interest and progress.

Under Abdul Aziz's reign, the people rejoiced, exactly how the book of Proverbs put it. The righteous ruler brings progress, improves the life of the people, builds infrastructures, creates jobs, and manages the nation's resources for the benefit of all. That is good governance and democracy.

One of his faithful slaves, Mazahim, once asked him, 'What did you leave for your children?' Abdul Aziz's reply was astonishing. Guess what he said. 'God.' Abdul Aziz shared what he had with the poor and needy. He had the power and authority to steal all the nation's wealth, just like our present-day African leaders; but because of his great faith in God, discipline, contentment, and lack of corrupt mind, he chose to serve the people instead.

I will propose to each and everyone who is a ruler or a public servant to first study and learn about the life and leadership attributes of this great man before ruling us. Abdul Aziz is a worthy character needed in our corrupt society today, where people's resources are being hijacked by a few greedy elements calling themselves our leaders and public servants. It is not too late—we can still learn from Abdul Aziz to improve and transform our attitude for the benefit of all.

The joys and benefits of having a righteous and quality leader with vision and love for the fatherland cannot be overemphasised. Good leaders are bound to make progress and move forward. Africa has been downgraded because of its lack of honest leaders with a patriotic mindset to serve the people or the governed. Our blessed continent has remained undeveloped for years because of the lack of genuine democratic principles and rule of law, abuse of power, and mainly corrupt practices, which have hampered growth and achievements in the areas of science, innovation, infrastructure, etc. Let us hope and work together to address these issues in order to move forward as others have done around the world.

CHAPTER 7

New Direction, Building Infrastructures, and Changing Politics

Change is always possible, either positive or negative. Africa, therefore, needs to change from its bad attitude to embrace a good and patriotic attitude in order to lift the continent out of poverty, war, and conflict coupled with political disaster. It needs to look towards the development of integrated infrastructure that will enhance the lives and mobility of its population. These will help in business, commerce, and international cooperation amongst nations, states, and citizenry. We are witnesses to what has taken place in China, India, Brazil, Qatar, and a lot of nations once known as third world nations. We should not be left out in making progress by our own doing; that is our inability to embrace a new way of living. The thinking of leaders and citizens should be more oriented towards 'we' than 'I'.

An individualistic mindset has long played a role in the way we live and do things; let us find a new approach to working together in the continent in the areas of education, science and technology, as well joint development projects.

This brings me to a lot of development ideals initiated by organisations such as NEPAD, PIDA, and Common Market for Eastern and Southern Africa (COMESA). If we as Africans can be genuine, realistic, and nationalistic in our approach of carrying out many of the joint initiatives with the amount of resources we have, we can overcome all odds and become a continent the world can look up to. The new direction we need is only to transform our way of life, change our political structure, embrace genuine democracy, and limit or reduce corruption in our system. The leaders of the people, police, army, and many officers of different institutions should serve and care for the people. Also, it shouldn't be about only them, their families, clans, tribesmen, and cronies. As we make these resolutions, adopt them, and live them, then we are heading to an upward movement and a better Africa, if I may say.

A new direction forward in Africa might include de-escalation and resolving of all conflict s in the continent. A joint initiative that will focus on resolving all violent conflicts, both ongoing and even imminent signs of new ones, should be tackled. Conflicts have helped a lot in derailing Africa; many of our resources have been misdirected in purchasing rejected and outdated arms by the West. The cases of Ethiopia and Eritrea are good examples of people suffering from the lack of food and healthcare. But billions of dollars were wasted on arms and ammunition to fight unnecessary battles that claimed both lives and properties.

The recent case of South Sudan has shown the need for Africa to shun conflicts and violent struggles that drain our meagre resources for development. The money spent on buying arms and ammunition can even be used to solve some issues regarding the distribution of resources to benefit all. If we learn to share resources equitably to all regions, province, states, etc., agitation that results in conflicts can be limited.

The new direction is economic development, integrating economic activities in the whole of Africa, where the issue of borders should be eliminated. The free flow of trade between African nations will empower a lot of people. Trade increase and the free movement of goods and services as well as people will generate revenues and funds amongst nations. Bob Marley said, 'A hungry man is an angry man.' Most of the conflicts and limitations in development in our continent are results of hunger, where people can't find work, even if they come with skills and education. The need to address these issues is quite overdue to help reduce violence and replace it with progress.

The new direction we need is also about changing the politics of the day, where so-called democracy has eluded the people. A new chapter has to be started, where the political leaders and civil society have to work together in letting the citizens of every state be part and parcel of democracy. Our citizenry need to be educated on the process of the democracy; they have to understand their rights and the obligations of the people who rule them. The importance of letting the people's vote count in every election is one of the greatest ways to uphold the principles of democracy. The policy of a one-party state is not democratic in the real sense. The use of intimidation and the harassment of opposition do not represent democracy, and a fraudulent election and malpractices during an election are against the principles of democracy.

Let democracy—the government of the people, by the people, and for the people—speak. By the time we embrace the culture of true democratic processes or practices, then we'll be heading to a new Africa, where new brains and creative young people will be part of the politics of the day. This will help us move forward and develop in a way that will impress the rest of the world. We are a great people, and we need to recognise that without genuine democracy in the continent, our desired future will still be far. The dividends of true nations will continue to elude us if we continue in a process where one man or party dominates power for twenty to thirty or more years. When this happens, they end up running short of ideas. The law of diminishing returns sets in; dictatorship will also set in with harsh and aggressive policies towards opposition and the citizens. The José Eduardo dos Santoses, Mugabes, Ben Alis, Mubaraks, and others like them begin to manifest.

A new direction may include turning the African economy into a productive economy rather than a consuming economy, relying on China, which is destroying a little manufacturing sector in the continent. We have to find a way to work together in building a productive economy since we have the natural resources. The primary raw materials are within our continent. We only have to buy or develop means to harness them ourselves or find a joint technical approach that will enable us to turn our raw materials into finished products. The idea of depending on the West and China for finished products has to be done away with if we really want to move forward as a continent. This will create jobs in our different nations and limit drastic unemployment affecting our youths. The process of building a productive sector of the economy it will lead to the development of infrastructure, which is one of the greatest problems facing the continent of Africa both now and in the near future if it is not tackled.

Infrastructure Development

Every now and then, you hear from the West and many African sycophants saying that, for example, Nigeria, Angola, or any other country in Africa has the fastest-growing economy. This has deceived a lot of these nations in the continent. Anyway, I don't know exactly what they are using to classify them as the fastest-growing economy, but the UN still sees them as places were the poverty level is high. The economies of many of these countries are nonproductive. They depend mainly on importation in main areas. The infrastructure in most of the nations in Africa is nothing to write home about. The erratic nature of the power supplies is sickening. There are no good roads and no railways. Means of communications are very bad and not highly developed. Infrastructure in terms of what is needed for a developing economy is not there. The oil industry most of them depend on is still run and controlled by the West. Most of their oil is refined outside their nations and returned to them for a certain price.

It is said that an inevitably thriving economy brings about demands for an expanded infrastructure. But we have not seen this kind of situation taking place in many of the nations in Africa. The so-called fastest-growing economy in Africa or whatever has a dilapidated network of roads and no new railways. Effective and massive communications technology connections are yet to be seen. In fact, most roads linking the refineries of Nigeria and Angola are nothing to talk well of. Linking the capitals to other areas of the nations is still problematic. You can have a smooth drive from the Netherlands to Spain, but that has not yet taken place in Africa, even between two neighbouring countries. Sometimes in a place like Nigeria, the so-called giant of Africa, to travel on road from Lagos to Port Harcourt is somehow a dangerous journey to make. BBC correspondents who travelled home in 2011 or 2012 with Chinua Achebe before he died can confirm what I am saying. They were witnesses to the nature of the roads in Nigeria.

In fact, if the economy is doing well, we want to see a reflection of it on the nation's infrastructure. We know it cannot take place in one day, but a sign of good things is always visible.

The development of infrastructure is of great demand and importance if the continent will move forward and develop to be on par with other developing nations around the world. Well-developed infrastructure will empower the citizens to become more creative and productive in many areas of life. Maybe it is good we define what is meant by 'infrastructure' so that many laymen can understand why some of these infrastructure are needed in every day of their life and how they can improve their day-to-day living.

Through the AU came about the idea and initiative to embark on infrastructural development in the continent. However, it is like the organ for this programme of integrated development in the areas of roads, telecommunications, ICT, schools, railways, etc. has been slow, if really happening at all. A new partnership for African development through NEPAD has been established to carry out infrastructural development in the continent of Africa for the benefit of the masses.

It is an AU strategic framework for Pan-African socioeconomic development. It is both a vision and a policy framework for Africa in the twenty-first century. NEPAD, at the beginning, was conceived as a radical intervention spearheaded by African leaders to address critical challenges facing the continent—poverty, development, and African marginalisation internationally. It was a well-thought-out, good idea that could have addressed most of the issues discussed in some earlier chapters of this work. However, it has turned out to be like all other African dreams that never come true. Since the inception of NEPAD, Africans are still waiting to reap the benefits of this great and noble idea, which can transform the continent of Africa.

The implementation of NEPAD's objectives is yet to materialise in the sense that the citizens of nations have not yet received or benefitted from those things NEPAD promised to deliver or usher in. NEPAD can provide a unique opportunity for African nations to take full control of their development agendas and work closely together and cooperate more effectively with international partners. Though we need to take control, we also need other nations to work with us; but it has to be on an equal basis, not with us as playing a subservient role. NEPAD's idea to manage a number of development projects is very important if we really want to meet the continent's goals in areas such as agriculture and food security, regional integration and infrastructure, human development, economic and corporate governance, and cross-cultural issues.

In fact, these are excellent idea that need urgent attention by Africans, and the leaders need to wake up to these issues if we are really looking for a way forward in the continent. For if these things are genuinely pursued and half realised, we will be on our way to liberate ourselves from the burdens facing the nations in Africa.

The process of working to realise NEPAD's objectives must be coupled with the consciousness of every African leader as well as the citizens themselves. Building an economy to meet the needs of the twenty-first century will be paramount in each and every mind. Infrastructural development is a major issue that has driven development in Africa to the ground since we have been unable to reach that goal of reliable and dependable infrastructure.

Infrastructural development in many areas as listed in NEPAD'S objectives will help us to become conscious in investing in areas like agriculture. Agriculture is a major area we need to build and invest in, in the continent in order to overcome food scarcity. Bob Marley said, 'A hungry man is an angry man.' When the people can feed themselves, they have the mindset to think, create, and work in building an organised society. Many advanced nations on the earth started developing from agriculture. Even US weapons development started from farmers working in the agricultural sector.

Building good infrastructure such as power and energy, good networks of roads and railway systems, ICT, and communications technology all work together to also improve food production. Many years back and in the present, many African nations have depended on food packets and supplies from other countries. Improved agricultural systems to improve food production have become possible because of good infrastructure and investment in the areas mentioned above. Let us not forget that Africa was good in irrigation in Egypt then. Irrigation is a greatly needed and urgent infrastructure in many nations in the continent. The seas and oceans that surround Africa are a good means for our leaders to think of investing in and building irrigation systems that can power our food production.

During the early 1960s, a worldwide war on hunger was the main purpose of agriculture, with a general attention on the growing food deficit. Today, in twenty-first century, many nations have escaped this threat; but African countries remain victims of hunger and food scarcity. This has happened because leaders have failed to develop infrastructures that will help in improving food production as well as enable areas of scarcity to receive food movement from areas with plenty.

For instance, since my time as a young boy growing up in the continent, I have not heard of food scarcity or starvation in the West African subregion. However, it is a different story when it comes to the East and Central African subregions. Ethiopia, for instance, has been hit many times with the problem of hunger and starvation because of lack of food.

Continuous lack of infrastructure in the continent has hampered development in many sectors of the economy. A good network of road and rail systems linking nations in the subregion will allow the movement of goods and services and reduce the cost of agricultural produce as well as finished products emanating from agriculture. Pineapples are mainly grown in Benin Republic, Gabon, etc. Juice and other products are produced from them, so we need an integrated system that will allow some of these products from areas of plenty to areas of little. This will enhance distribution and limit lack in some areas.

Seeing that Africa is blessed with good weather conditions, agriculture should be a major source of the economy. The United States, for example, despite its harsh and sometimes difficult weather, is still the biggest food producer in the world. In fact, leaders and citizens of Africa should look at agriculture beyond subsistence agriculture, which has been and remains the system of agriculture in Africa. Agriculture is a source of many industries. Through them, a great number of infrastructures and mass employment opportunities can develop. Mechanised agriculture is what we need in the continent if food security and peace will be achieved. This will help in development in many areas of society. By the time we mechanise our agricultural sector, we will be able to eradicate poverty, violence, and conflict. When our youths are gainfully employed, they will have less chances of being used by those who cause trouble. Their involvement in terrorism will also be limited.

Energy and Power Supply

No nation has developed without being able to enhance its source of energy and power supply. Industrial development, communications, mechanised agriculture, ICT, and rail and road transport can never exists in isolation. Most of these infrastructures are linked and interdependent. Energy and power supply will power all and most activities geared towards sustainable development.

The regular supply of energy and power in any given state is the highest source of industrial revolution, in which activities towards building a sound industrial base are centred. This is why a country like the United States sees energy and power as a 'national security' issue. The dilapidated and erratic nature of energy and power supply in many nations in the continent of Africa has affected infrastructural development that is sustainable over time. In fact, many of the political leaders in Africa do not take this problem into account; and in fact, many of them have never seen it as a major setback in Africa's movement forward. If they had, the great amount of wealth laundered out of the continent to the West would have been invested in this area.

The failure of many nations in Africa to provide power and energy to their citizenry has also contributed to the lack of quality and sustainable infrastructure. Schools and hospitals are run and managed using generating sets. This affects the quality of services provided by these institutions and even increases costs and passes the burden to the final consumers of the services these institutions provide. For instance, a country like Nigeria has been unable to provide a regular supply of power and energy to its citizens since the British left. This kills productivity as well as talents. There have been cases in this country where the power went out during surgical operations in hospitals, and doctors had to manage generating sets to try to do their work of saving lives. But this a country where one politician or public officer will steal billion of dollars and hide it in foreign account instead of the state investing this money in energy and power in order to improve lives. The nature of this problem has lasted years, so something drastic needs to be done to address it. Infrastructural development is a thing that every reasonable leader should invest in. This will improve lives, open doors for investments, and create employment.

NEPAD should call to action the leaders and those who thought of this vision of continental infrastructural development in Africa so that it can be a reality. Integrated infrastructure in the continent will be a power engine to our breaking away from poverty and emerging as a continent of the future. China has survived today because she focused on most of the things discussed in this book as well as some of the visions of NEPAD. The implementation has to be fast and steady as well as realistic and focused on achieving the visions.

As a developing and emerging economy, the continent of Africa cannot survive or sustain its population without serious investments in infrastructure in the area of energy and power supply. We all know that energy is inevitable for human life; a secure and accessible supply of energy and power is critical for the sustainability of modern societies. For centuries, fossil fuels have been the main source of energy supply but are now facing challenges and depletion due to a number of factors.

Therefore, renewable energy sources such as solar, wind, biomass, etc. are new areas of investments to provide a sustainable supply of energy for societal use and industrial purposes. Africa has to look towards this area of infrastructural development in order to provide her with sustainable energy the society needs for development.

The European Union has embarked on building a mass solar energy project in the deserts of Africa while the continental leaders sit and watch. Tomorrow, they will be buying this energy at a high cost from Europe. This should be a sign for them to also look for investments in this area or other areas of renewable energy where they have resources to harness energy supplies for the future. Let us make haste while the sun shines for the future of our continent's development and progress.

Transportation

Developing transportation infrastructure in the continent of Africa is one area where great urgency is needed. An integrated transport system connecting nations and linking major cities and rural areas will help improve lives and increase the movement of goods and services amongst the continental people. The free movement of people and business across borders with fewer impediments due to the lack of a quality transport network linking states and nations will usher in economic growth in the continent. Let us assume that there are railway lines connecting Southern Africa, Western Africa, Central and Northern Africa as well. Then the continental citizens can interact with one another in many areas daily. Trade, commerce, and intercultural activities will improve. This will minimise or remove the fears each person has against himself or herself. Accessing information can be easier since there is a possibility of being able to reach each capital on a daily basis or in a few days.

I am impressed by the actions and approach taken by ECOWAS in its activities on many fronts. In the last two to three years, she has been busy with a road project connecting Nigeria to Benin Republic and Togo to Ghana. In fact, this is a well-thought-out idea that will yield dividends in due time. People and businesses can easily move amongst these neighbouring West African nations. This is exactly what we are referring to when we talk about an integrated network of roads and railways linking our different capitals.

The lack of integrated networks of roads, railways, and waterways hinders and hampers travel and the movement of people, goods, and services amongst neighbouring nations. If we are able to build infrastructures to take care of these areas of transport, the benefits will be enormous. There will be great improvements in trade, commerce, communications, and internations corporation, which will create a conducive climate for progress in many areas of life in the continent. While searching for materials for this work on integrated infrastructures in Africa, I happened to stumble on the PIDA and its agenda on infrastructure development in Africa. In fact, it was like an expo because the ideas fell into the contents of this book. The Programme for Infrastructure Development in Africa (PIDA) needs money and technocrats that can genuinely work to make this dream a reality. According to PIDA, it needs up to $11,391,527 to help it carry out its project of building infrastructures in of Africa. To some, you may wonder how they can raise this money to carry out their objectives. But don't forget that African leaders have more than such an amount in Western banks.

Anyway, what we need is practice and not so much paperwork, which is never realised in the end. Let's go back to the problem of transport infrastructure development, which is highly needed in the continent. Africa has a lot of waterways in which we have to invest in order to develop it for the good of the people. If our waterways are developed, the cost of transport will be reduced; and many will no longer rely only on road transport, which is more or less the only affordable means of transport to many in the continent.

The urgency in this area of infrastructure development in Africa cannot continue to wait if we are going to move forward. In Western Europe, all these means of transport are available to the citizens, and they can choose the most cost-effective to use. This makes life easy for the citizens and increases the movement of people, goods, and services, which also benefits the state in the long run. Taxes are collected when people make purchases of tickets to enjoy these services, and this in turn benefits the states.

It is unfortunate that many nations in Africa have no national carriers that can fly around the world. Many Africans leaving the continent spend their money patronising other continental airlines because many of their nations have none. A joint African airline that can fly around the world or within the continent at a cost-effective price can help improve the lives of its citizens and benefit the continent at large. Imagine a country like Nigeria without a national carrier. In fact, the Nigerian citizens living outside the borders flying every day could afford to maintain a national carrier if there were any. Many international air carriers such as KLM, Lufthansa, Iberia, and Emirates fly in and out of Nigeria almost every day. Can you imagine how much they realise from Nigerians alone to talk of the rest of the continent? So why don't Africans think and use their God-given brains like the others? I hope and believe that leaders as well as other citizens will use their brains in the right sense for the good and benefit of us all.

Other Areas of Infrastructure Development

Infrastructure development is not limited to the major ones mentioned above; there are still many areas where the need for infrastructure cannot be neglected.

In the beginning of this book, we spoke of how better, efficient, and effective our institutions need to be. In the context of infrastructure development in Africa, we also have to recognise that institutions such as health, schools, prisons, and others need and demand better, quality, and durable infrastructure that can help the personnel discharge their duties effectively and grant them the chance to deliver. Without sound infrastructure, most of the institutions will not function as expected in the professional level. The areas of infrastructure in schools, health sector, and prison services all require advanced technology to work with. This is why it is also of paramount importance that governments in Africa invest in the development of communications technology and computer literacy programmes for workers. For instance, a young man in Kenya has been able to save lives through childbearing by employing communications and computer technology in serving local and rural women. He established Telemed, a foundation that can reach pregnant women in the local areas through mobile telephones linked to a computer programme the young man developed. He returned to Kenya after graduating from Clinton Global Initiative University in the United States.

This is the kind of projects our political leaders have to embrace and invest in so that they can be a model for all African nations in terms of healthcare services. There is a lot of innovation going on today in the health sector as well as in education, and these innovations cannot work without the basic infrastructures needed to support and sustain them.

We are all aware that infrastructure can't exist out of the blue. Money is needed to finance building infrastructure in any given place around the world. Without money, PIDA's plan cannot be realised even though it is a noble plan. Individual nations working jointly with the AU cannot achieve anything as well without money and the determination to realise their vision.

Many nations in the continent are rich and have resources to build the infrastructures we need; but the problem lies in the will, management, and honesty to serve the people. It is quite understandable for people to know that without money, these things will merely remain as nice dreams for lack of implementation. Implementation is possible if financial institutions such as banks will finance some of these projects through loans and funds that can be paid back. According to information from PIDA, the African Union Commission (AUC), NEPAD secretariats, and the banks are involved; and AUC is playing a leading role in PIDA's initiative. The ADB and other international aid organisations should be consulted to finance and be part of this noble idea that will help Africa come out of poverty and advance for a better future. In fact, I would prefer if the aid of Western nations to many African countries be channelled towards realising this goal of infrastructural development in Africa rather than giving it to politicians who will later return the money as offshore funds hidden in various Western banks.

Since the objective of PIDA is to attend to one of the greatest needs of the citizens of the African continent and businesses, then it is important that every party in the continent support the efforts. Corporate bodies and entrepreneurs as well as governments should participate in making this dream a reality. If Africa will be able to tackle some of the issues discussed in this work, it will be on its way to improving socioeconomic problems and eradicating or reducing the poverty level. If some of the issues are managed, enhanced, and taken care of by the AU, NEPAD, PIDA, and others, then the sun will rise in the continent; the rate of accelerated development that will occur will surprise the pessimists of Africa. Individual nations should also look at the objectives of bodies such COMESA, ECOWAS, ECOMOG, NEPAD, and others and start to implement some of their ideas in their respective countries in order to give hope to its citizens that a better life is under way.

We have spoken about education in the previous chapters, but infrastructure for a quality and better schooling environment cannot be left out in the area of development. Technocrats needed to manage and maintain infrastructures are produced through quality education and raising graduates that can compete with their peers at an international level. Education is a way out of poverty. It helps in integration and improves people's way of life; it also makes people open-minded, ready to assimilate and embrace other cultures.

Education is the door to emancipation from a lot of ill-conceived opinions and prejudices that create hatred and breeds violence and conflict. We, therefore, need to invest in education so as to empower our citizens. It was mostly education in the West that granted the early African nationalists the opportunity to work towards liberating Africa from the shackles of colonialism. But since our present leaders have turned themselves into the likes of the colonial masters, we, therefore, need education to create informed and liberal minds to stand and oppose those who stand in the way of Africa's progress and development. Education enlightens the mind and therefore serves a lot of purposes in health-related matters. More education means a better way of life and keeping up with hygiene, which reduces the chances of contracting many diseases.

Infrastructure in water resources and provision needs urgent action in many areas of the continent. Many do not have access to pure drinking water, and where it exists, it is sometimes limited to the population present. The citizens of a given state have the right to energy, security, and pipe-borne water for the state to provide. In Africa, most of the leaders take these human rights issues for granted. Let this piece awaken their conscience to their obligations to the citizens. Building infrastructure and institutions to take care of some of these issues will be the pathway for the continent to move forward, becoming a modern society fit for the twenty-first century.

In fact, the pages of this book cannot contain all the burdens and demands of the citizens of the great continent of Africa. This work is just a little extract to hopefully awaken some of us—mostly our so-called leaders—from sleep. Our leaders should take think about it mostly as humans and then as fathers of the nations that they have to provide for their family. We are their children, and they are governing us. Therefore, a father that does not take care of his responsibilities in the household is said to be irresponsible. So let them take care of the nation's family under them.

Changing Politics

The idea of a political system in Africa has to be changed towards democratising the nations in the continent instead of turning them more and more into dictatorships. The more a country becomes democratic, the more civil, ethical, moral, and progressive it becomes. We are witnesses to what has happened in most of the Latin and South American nations as they learned to hate dictatorship and chose democracy. Their society has become more civil; economically, most of them have emerged from poverty. Under Luiz Inácio Lula da Silva, about 12,000,000 of Brazilians were lifted out of poverty into the middle class within eight years of his administration. Mahathir Mohamad of Malaysia was able to transform his country to a modern economy within twenty years in power. Many African nations (e.g. Nigeria and Ghana) were richer than Malaysia, say, in the late 1970s and the early 1980s. Today, many citizens of these African countries are languishing in Malaysian prisons for petty crimes. Due to the harsh situations in the continent, many have migrated there, searching for a better life. Yet our leaders claim that they are democratic in nature and have chosen democracy.

The politics of a one-party state, dictatorship, corruption, neglect of citizens, and abuse of power have to change for good in order to move the continent forward. A policy of inclusive rather than exclusive should be copied from other developed nations around the world so as to limit and avoid conflict that is tearing us apart. The tribal kleptocracy has to give way to a government oriented towards transparency, accountability, and innovation with attention to human rights and leaders realising their obligations to their citizens.

I remember former president Barack Obama saying that no nation is going to create wealth if its leaders exploit the economy for enriching themselves. So in terms of change in politics, are your leaders or public officers thinking of abandoning the idea of enriching themselves with our resources? If we choose to build a genuine democracy geared towards transforming our continent, we have to abandon the old ways of doing things, knowing that the strength of our democracy can help advance human rights for people everywhere in Africa. Real democracy is a government that respects the will of its own people and that governs by consent and not by coercion. The government with this attitude is more stable and more successful than governments that without (Barack Obama). In fact, this is the new direction we need and the new type of politics we are demanding in the continent of Africa.

However, it will not come in a plate of gold. If those in power refuse to choose this direction, then let us form a common front and move them to act, or let us drive them away or make the seat too hot for them to stay there for so long, as they have been doing. The leaders of the continent should not forget that capable, reliable, and transparent institutions are a key to success—strong parliaments, honest police forces, independent judges, a free and fair press, and a vibrant private sector. These are things that give life to democracy—of course, that is what matters in people's everyday life (Barack Obama).

In these pages of this book, a lot has been said about transparency, good governance, the treatment of people with justice, and respect for human rights. In fact, I give a small account of the life of a once-righteous leader by the name of Umar bin Abdul Aziz of Haman in Egypt, who ruled with justice and righteousness. How his people enjoyed and rejoiced when he ruled. As a leader, this is your turn to emulate Aziz for the good of your people.

Changing politics in the continent also means that the African nations should also develop and have strong and quality foreign policy. It is as though many of the countries in Africa have no foreign policy standard. It is a continent where other foreign nations come in and do what they like in the market, harnessing the resources of the continent. For example, Nigeria—as big as she claims to be—looks like she has no foreign policy objectives. Her citizens get molested outside, but she takes little or no step to address the issue. Millions of naira were wasted in Liberia, Sierra Leone, Angola, etc., without any benefit. That is why they call the USA a bad name because America will not waste resources like that without considering the benefits in terms of foreign policy and national security interest. This is also an area many African nations have to look into in order to have leverage in certain circumstances. In particular, in dealing with China, foreign policy and national security interest have to be thoroughly evaluated in the long term, not only looking at the present state.

Let leaders of the continent join hands to build an integrated market, infrastructure, sustainable development, and a strong economy as well as to reduce conflict through creating equality and human rights for all. This will bring peace and the change we need to move Africa forward.

CONCLUSION

I appreciate the time you devoted to read through the pages of this book. In fact, it will be more important if each and every one of us understands what is the most vivid truth pointed out here. Act on it in your own little way to bring about the positive change we need to make Africa a progressive continent.

Much has been said, described, and spoken of; but if actions do not follow words, then there will be no headway. Continental Africa has suffered from slavery, colonial maltreatment, economic strangulations, protracted conflicts, as well as poverty and disease. We are not the only continent that went through tough times, though ours were more because of Eurocentrism, Arab expansion and influence, etc. However, we still survived. So this is the time for us to toughen up and march on to overcome the new challenges facing us, even though some were created by our political brothers.

Building a new Africa by employing most of the ideas enumerated in this work and that of many others—including implementing the visions of NEPAD, PIDA, COMESA, and a host of other beneficial ideas—will be crucial to our new nature. China has survived, emerged, and woken up from where she was lying as a sleeping giant for centuries before now. We can do the same if the great conscious awakening comes to all our minds. The need for stronger ties amongst nations, regions, tribes, and clans will help us forge ahead in realising a new Africa, where demarcation created by outsiders through politics, religion, etc. will be a thing of the past. It might sound impossible, but it is also prophetic—if, and only if, our political leaders will realise that it is not better for them to die in overseas hospitals because they are unable to build quality, standard, and sustainable institutions and infrastructure at home that can care for them and their citizens at any time.

We should strive for an Africa that is well grounded in sustainable infrastructure, strong and reliable institutions, ending and resolving impending conflicts, and making sure to mediate in conflict before it gets out of the hand. The sun will rise for better days for the continent. Let leaders learn how to guide and build up people instead of dominating, intimidating, and harassing them—the worst way to rule over people, which some of them resisted and fought against during the colonial days. We should aim for an Africa where the new generations are given the opportunity to be educated and to be able to compete and participate in the governing and developing of a type of society that is equitable and inclusive in nature. This will limit agitation, violence, wars, and poverty, including disease and death. The economic effects and benefits of all these will be immensurable to quantify and will be enjoyed by the continent and the rest of the world.

Let us join hands and work collectively to make it possible to move Africa forward. The future generations are the most important people to keep in mind so that what has befallen this generation will not happen to them. It has been said that united we stand, divided we fall. The division that was created by those who partitioned Africa should blind and overshadow our mission of integrating Africa into a common fold that will hold us further together for our betterment.

REFERENCES

Types of Schools
https://www.slideshare.net
https://www.gov.uk

Types of Education
Asst. Prof. Y. N. Mshake, Motiwala College of Educational Sciences,
    Moshi, Maharashtra

Importance of Education
www.thehungerproject.org.uk
www.zapineta.uk

History of American Presidents
https://www.loc.gov/

The Right to Education: Article 2 of the First Protocol of the
    European Convention on Human Rights (1952)

No Child Left Behind Act of George W. Bush, former president of
    the United States

New African magazine (October 2008), extracts from Akinyi von
    K'Orinda-Yimbo

Samuel Estwick's memorandum to Lord Mansfield

W. J. Perry, *The Growth of Civilization* (1924)

World Health Organization's 2007 report on healthcare

Wayande's study 2003, 1992 (page 20)

Barack Obama's speech to the African Union, Addis Ababa (July 2015)

G. Elliot Smith, *The Ancient Egyptians and the Origin of Civilization* (1911)

John K. Galbraith, *The New Industrial State* (1967)

www.ingramcontent.com/pod-product-compliance
Lightning Source LLC
Chambersburg PA
CBHW020526290526
45786CB00002B/771